60009 UN[...]
SOUTH AFRICA
Stories from the Support Crew

Michael Mather (editor)

AMBERLEY

Dedicated to the memory of Lindsay, Davy, Herbert & DJ.

All profits from this book will go to various Scottish railway preservation projects.

Front cover: On a sunny 17 April 1981, Number 9 stands outside its shed at Markinch. (Michael Mather)

Back cover: Number 9 departs York in style on 30 November 1985 with a Cumbrian Mountain Express for Carlisle. (Geoff Green, Davy Murray Collection)

First published 2021

Amberley Publishing
The Hill, Stroud
Gloucestershire, GL5 4EP

www.amberley-books.com

Copyright © Michael Mather, 2021

The right of Michael Mather to be identified as the Author
of this work has been asserted in accordance with the
Copyrights, Designs and Patents Act 1988.

British Library Cataloguing in Publication Data.
A catalogue record for this book is available from the British Library.

ISBN 978 1 4456 8275 4 (print)
ISBN 978 1 4456 8276 1 (ebook)

Typesetting by Aura Technology and Software Services, India.
Printed in Great Britain.

Foreword
by Dr John Cameron CBE

I have had the great pleasure of working with the various support crews of Number 9 for over fifty years, and what fun and experiences we have had during that period.

From my first visit to see Number 9 at Ferryhill depot in Aberdeen, where the knowledgeable Foreman Fitter – the late Jock Tosh, a real railway character – informed me that Number 9 was without doubt the best of the A4s still running, Number 9 and the support crews have been a big part of my life.

Even at the negotiation to purchase Number 9 those involved were all so helpful. The chief stores controller in Buchanan House, as it was then, informed me that only 'registered metal dealers' could purchase old locomotives. He then asked if I had any machinery. I replied I only had 'tractors and combines' whereupon he replied 'OK you are a metal dealer!'

From Aberdeen, Number 9 came to Thornton depot in Fife before going to the last 2 miles of the former recently closed East Fife Central freight line, which very conveniently was situated within the boundary of one of my farms.

So, for six years, Number 9 operated in steam on summer Sundays with its one carriage observation coach. The track was only on ash ballast and moved dramatically every time the loco passed over – how it never came off the road I'll never know.

Then in the early 1970s British Rail relented, allowing certain certified steam locos back on the main line – and so Number 9 made another journey by road, this time to Ladybank and back on to the main line. The rest is history!

Over a lifetime of memories two stand out in particular. Firstly, Number 9's first run in 'private ownership' while at Thornton depot en route to Lochty, when Number 9 returned to Perth to haul Scottish Region's 'Farewell to Steam' special in 1967 from Perth to Aberdeen. Along with a Stanier Class 5 they hauled a mammoth train of eighteen coaches over the scheduled 85 miles in 83 minutes!

The second unfading memory was in 2015 for the opening of the Borders Line, where Number 9 successfully hauled the royal train conveying HM the Queen from Waverley to Tweedbank for the opening ceremony.

Now both Number 9 and myself are going quietly into retirement! But none of these memories could have been possible without the willing participation of the various members of the support crew, to whom I am eternally grateful.

John Cameron

Introduction

By the time this book is published, A4 Pacific Number 60009 *Union of South Africa*, or Number 9 as it is generally referred to, will have come to the end of its lengthy main line career, having worked almost continuously since 1937.

We, the support crew, have decided to mark the occasion by compiling this book of stories, reminiscences and photographs of our times with the locomotive, the ups and downs of main line operation, the good and not so good times, and the fun we have had over many years.

Many members have come and gone over the years, some sadly passing away, and although we now only have one original member from when John Cameron bought the locomotive from British Railways in 1966, the main core of the crew have been involved since the 1970s and 1980s, all mostly living within a few miles of Markinch in Fife – Number 9's long-time home. It is these members who have largely contributed to this book.

We are not just a support crew, but friends as well, sharing other interests and meeting socially. Along with our regular Monday night meetings, the highlights of the year are the annual Christmas party, and of course the Burns supper. Trips by car down to the Settle to Carlisle railway to photograph steam specials and weekends away to the Severn Valley autumn gala, among other places, also happened. When Number 9 was under overhaul and therefore not running for many months we could be found on Monday evenings or Sundays hill walking or perhaps following the course of a long-closed railway. The one requirement on these walks was that there had to be a nearby pub at the end.

During the twenty years Number 9 was based at Markinch, after finishing work for the night we would adjourn to The Bethune Arms, or The Beth as we called it. Later, when it closed, we went to Jamie's Bar, known to us as Messerschmitt's – after the German landlord who had taken the surname of Smith. Both pubs had photographs of Number 9 on their walls.

Being on a support crew in recent years has been a time-consuming business, especially for us, with the distance we often had to cover just to get to the engine. Gone were the days of turning up on a Saturday morning, doing the days trip to, say, Aberdeen and back, and being home at night. For most of the tours that ran in England it was a minimum of three days away from home coupled with long car or rail journeys, and some of these journeys became memorable in themselves for many reasons.

Juggling work, home, and family life could be a challenge, although this became easier as one by one we retired from full-time work. Thankfully for the tours south of the border we have been assisted by a large group of support crew volunteers from all over England.

In recent years, with so many tours and the introduction of more regulations and health and safety guidelines, organising repairs and maintenance by approved engineers at approved locations, and the paperwork all this entailed, it became increasingly difficult to carry this out part-time, and so Fraser took on this full-time role. This made life easier for everyone.

The support crew pose in front of Number 9 at Bounds Green depot, London, prior to the locomotive working the Elizabethan to Peterborough on 29 October 1994. Standing, from left: Mike, Fraser, Graeme, Marilyn, John and Davy. Kneeling: Colin and Nick. (David Murray)

Over the years we have met many people who are fans of our engine, not just enthusiasts, but also the general public. It was always gratifying to see so many out to see us pass by, young and old alike, smiling and waving.

John Cameron is at the regulator and waving his cap to the onlookers on the loading bank, as Number 9 flys through Markinch station on a cold frosty Saturday morning in November 1980. (Michael Mather)

There are many stories we could tell and those in the following pages are only a fraction of what we could have used. The same goes for the photographs, most of which we have drawn from our own collections, and also from the extensive collection of our dear departed friend and colleague Davy Murray. We have used as many of his photographs as possible.

We hope you enjoy what we have put together in this book and that it gives a feeling for what it is like to be a main line steam locomotive support crew member, and we thank everyone who has travelled with us the length and breadth of the country.

Michael Mather

LNER and BR Days

The first A4s, designed by Sir Nigel Gresley, were introduced in 1935.

It was June 1937 when *Union of South Africa* exited Doncaster Works. She was originally to be named *Osprey* but, in order to commemorate the coronation of King George VI, Gresley offered to name the five A4s ready to leave the works after the Commonwealth nations – Australia, New Zealand, India, South Africa and Canada. The naming ceremony for Number 9 took place on 28 June 1937 at Kings Cross.

Her first loaded test run took place on 20 June 1937 between Kings Cross and Cambridge, a regular testing route for Gresley's new Pacifics. She was destined to be a Scottish engine throughout her working life, and arrived at Haymarket within a few days to work an up Kings Cross at the end of June 1937. Her regular working was originally the Coronation Express and she first appeared on the Flying Scotsman in 1939 on the Newcastle–Edinburgh section. Number 9 was also seen on the Queen of Scots before hauling the inaugural up Capitals Express in 1950. This eventually became the non-stop Elizabethan service between Kings Cross and Edinburgh. Number 9 was provided with a corridor tender, so this became her regular service.

On the Elizabethan her claim to fame is that she hauled the longest known distance for this trip. This occurred on 6 September 1954 when there was flooding on the line north of Newcastle. The up service to Kings Cross had managed to traverse the problem

At the head of the train it was built and named to haul, and carrying its original number, 4488, *Union of South Africa* departs Newcastle Central with the up Coronation Express for London Kings Cross sometime in the late 1930s. This train ceased to run following the outbreak of the Second World War in 1939. (Colour-Rail)

In 1947, the year before the railways were nationalised, the LNER carried out a renumbering of all its locomotives into a more organised manner, and this is when Number 9 became Number 9! The loco is seen here sitting on the turntable at its home depot, Edinburgh Haymarket, in 1947 or early 1948 prior to receiving its final number, 60009, in May of that year. (R. K. Blencowe Collection)

before it became too severe, but Number 9 on the down service was not going to make it through. The train was diverted at Newcastle to Carlisle and ultimately to Edinburgh. This increased the distance travelled by some 30 miles. It was suggested that the run was completed non-stop but, as there were no water troughs north of Darlington, it is unlikely that this was the case. However, we do know that the run was completed without a further supply of coal. This was down to good work from both driver and fireman.

During the early 1960s her main work was in Scotland, working occasional Edinburgh–Aberdeen services, but mainly Glasgow–Aberdeen 3-hour expresses. Many of the trains she worked had names such as St Mungo, Aberdonian and Grampian expresses. She did, however, manage occasional forays south of the border and was the last A4 in regular service to work a train out of Kings Cross on 24 October 1964. This was the Jubilee Requiem to Newcastle and return. On the journey back to Kings Cross she was recorded as exceeding 95 mph and arrived in London more than 20 minutes early!

Throughout her time with LNER & BR she achieved the highest mileage in service, not far short of 2 million miles! She carried three different numbers – originally 4488, before being renumbered 9 in 1947, and 60009 in BR days. She had four different colour schemes – Garter Blue, Black, BR Blue and BR Brunswick Green.

Sadly, Number 9 was withdrawn at Aberdeen Ferryhill MPD on 1 June 1966 but was saved from the scrapyard by John Cameron, a Fife farmer who had a lifelong love of steam. Number 9 was chosen partly because she had been the last A4 to receive a

Three of Haymarket's seven A4s line up with four of the depot's Top Link drivers: Nos 60024 *Kingfisher*, 60004 *William Whitelaw* and 60009 *Union of South Africa*. From the left, the drivers are: Tony MacLeod, star of the British Transport film *The Elizabethan Express*; Bill MacLeod; Jimmy Swan; and Bill Paterson. This 1950s view was taken before the locomotives were fitted with Kylchap double chimneys in 1957/8. (LPR)

Hauling the Edinburgh to London Kings Cross non-stop train it is most associated with, The Elizabethan, Number 9 hurries through Grantham with the up service on 29 August 1961. (Colour-Rail)

complete overhaul. It was common for locos undergoing overhaul to be parted from their tender and Number 9 was no different. She was noted with several different tenders and ended up with a non-corridor version. Or did she? The loco was towed to Thornton MPD in Fife on 9 September 1966, with the corridor tender originally coupled to the 'Hush Hush'.

In order to avoid prying eyes, including schoolboy trainspotters, she was initially hidden from sight in a long single-road shed called the snakepit. This had been used during the war to inspect and prep locos, out of sight of German aircraft who may spot the glow from the fire.

As a final fling, Number 9 was to complete a run from Perth to Aberdeen on 25 March 1967, double-heading with Black 5 44997 on an eighteen-coach train. In order to ensure that she looked her best, the members of Thornton Model Railway Club, run by railwaymen for themselves and their families, volunteered to clean many years of soot, oil and grime that had accumulated. This, in fact, was the birth of the support crew as we know it today!

Black as coal, covered in grease
She'd served her country well
Soon to be once more set free
Resurrected from the dead.
A brand-new start with her gleaming coat
In all her majesty
Prepared by lads who 'spotted' her
To serve another day.

Number 9 was to leave BR metals in April 1967 but the story continues.

Colin Cant

Memories of the Glasgow–Aberdeen 3-hour Trains

The story of how Number 9 survived into preservation goes back to the early sixties. At that time dieselisation was in full swing and the A4 Pacifics on the Eastern Region were being withdrawn or relocated due to the introduction of the powerful Deltic diesel locomotives.

In Scotland some of the services were diesel-hauled, notably in the hands of the North British Locomotive (NBL) Type 2s, but these had proved to be extremely unreliable. The locomotives were fitted with German MAN engines, which had been built by NBL under licence.

In view of these problems, the general manager of the Scottish Region, James Ness, decided to introduce faster 3-hour trains between Glasgow and Aberdeen using the displaced A4 Pacifics.

So, in February 1962, A4 No. 60031 *Golden Plover* was transferred from Edinburgh Haymarket to Glasgow St Rollox. A trial run was arranged, but unfortunately the engine failed with a hot centre big end. Another A4, No. 60027 *Merlin*, recently ex-works from Doncaster, was used for the trial on 22 February 1962 and proved that these locomotives were more than up to the job.

Initially these two engines were used on the Glasgow to Dundee trains, until May/June when A4s Nos 60004 *William Whitelaw*, 60009 *Union of South Africa*, and 60011 *Empire of India* were transferred from Haymarket to Aberdeen Ferryhill.

The new accelerated trains began at the start of the summer timetable and No. 60011 *Empire of India* hauled the first southbound service from Aberdeen on 18 June 1962.

The four 3-hour trains were as follows: 7.10 a.m. Aberdeen–Glasgow (The Bon Accord); 5.30 p.m. Glasgow–Aberdeen (The Saint Mungo); 8.25 a.m. Glasgow–Aberdeen (The Grampian); and 5.15 p.m. Aberdeen–Glasgow (The Granite City).

I did not keep records in the early days, but I remember that engines 60009 and 60011 were used regularly on the 5.30 p.m. from Glasgow for the first year or so. Then one night, 26 November 1963, No. 60010 *Dominion of Canada* turned up. This was an ex-Kings Cross engine and the first of the nine English A4s that were to operate the 3-hour trains. Coming completely out of the blue, the excitement was like winning the lottery!

Over the four-year period that the 3-hour trains ran there were many highs and lows. One particular low occurred in 1963 when it was announced that NBL Type 2 No. D6123 would be re-engined by Paxman with a Valenta engine in an attempt to improve performance and reliability. After a lengthy evaluation period the locomotive began to appear more and more on the 8.25 Glasgow–Aberdeen and the 5.15 p.m. return. This was a St Rollox turn and it has to be said that there was always a bit of hostility towards the Gresley engines from some of the Glasgow men.

All told, sixteen A4 Pacifics were used at one time or another on the 3-hour trains and fourteen were allocated to Aberdeen Ferryhill. It was hardly surprising that enthusiasts came from all over the country to travel on these trains and enjoy some fast runs behind these famous locomotives.

The highlight for me over this period was the purchase of a Freedom of Scotland ticket during the school summer holidays of 1964. All told I had twenty-four runs behind engines 4, 6, 9, 16 and 26 during this holiday. As an example, one day consisted of the following: 60026, Stirling to Aberdeen (Morning Postal); 60009, Aberdeen to

Left: Following arrival at Glasgow Buchanan Street station with a train from Aberdeen, I was lucky enough to get a footplate ride up to St Rollox shed on Number 9, where it would be turned and serviced. This is the view from the footplate as 9 eases onto the turntable. (Nick Swierklanski)

Below: Number 9 is coaled at St Rollox's manual coaling stage. The Springbok plaque on the boiler side was a gift from a South African newspaper proprietor in the 1950s. (Nick Swierklanski)

Larbert 1.30 p.m (ex-Aberdeen); 60010, Stirling to Perth 5.30 p.m. (ex-Glasgow); 60016 Perth to Glasgow 5.15 p.m. (ex-Aberdeen).

Some of the timings of these trains were such that you could arrive at a station behind one A4, run to another platform and depart behind another.

My favourite journey was from Stirling to Perth, a stiff climb to Kinbuck, and a fast run down from Gleneagles. Number 9 was always a sterling performer and I can still remember the fireworks displays as the engine roared through the tunnel before Dunblane. The volcanic sparks bouncing off the tunnel roof and down the side of the train were a good simulation of re-entry in a space shuttle!

Once past Gleneagles the engine would be well notched up, the roar from the chimney would subside into a gentle purr and the engine would take off. At high speed you could tell that an A4 just wanted to go; it was all so effortless. Too soon it was time to slow down for Hilton Junction, through Moncrieff tunnel, past Perth locomotive depot and on into the station. As the train came to a stand, the dedicated train timers would emerge excitedly comparing notes. If you were lucky you could catch another A4 back to Stirling and do it all in reverse.

My best run from Stirling to Perth was with No. 60024 *Kingfisher* in August 1965 when we broke the 90 mph barrier on the run down From Gleneagles!

With the re-engining of No. D6123 proving successful, further members of the class had this work carried out and as time went on the number of A4s in service reduced until by April 1966 there were only four active. These were Nos 60009, 60019, 60024 and 60034.

Surprisingly, the 7.10 a.m. ex-Aberdeen was now diesel-hauled, whereas the 8.25 a.m. ex-Glasgow had returned to steam. The other train that was consistently A4-hauled was the 1.30 p.m. Aberdeen to Glasgow and 11 p.m. return. This was not a 3-hour timing, but had more stops, thus allowing enthusiastic drivers ample opportunity to demonstrate the acceleration of their steeds.

Number 9 was withdrawn on 1 June 1966 and remained at Ferryhill until the end came for the class in September of that year.

To mark the event, a special train was run on 3 September 1966 on the usual 3-hour timings from Glasgow to Aberdeen and return, hauled by No. 60019 *Bittern*.

This was advertised as the 'last run on the railway system of an A4 Pacific locomotive' and cost the princely sum of 40 shillings. However, the actual last run took place on 13 September when No. 60024 *Kingfisher*, deputising for a failed diesel, hauled the 5.15 p.m. from Aberdeen to Glasgow and returned the next day on the 8.25 a.m.

Fortunately, this was not the end as the immortal Number 9 has continued to delight enthusiasts for over fifty years. Little did I know at the time that twenty years after Number 9 was withdrawn from BR service, I would become a member of the support crew.

Nick Swierklanski

Reminiscence: Sixty Thousand and Nine

An author once wrote that a passing train
Was enough to confuse a strong man's brain
The guilty I am, for in my time
I've raced through Britain's hail and shine
Exalted, praised, my sheer delight
Admired by all along the line

A child of Sir Nigel's brain am I
A creature of strength and beauty fore by
As graceful as bird, as swift as light
Steaming and hauling through the night
I've seen the dawn of many a day
The Gresley knock in my side rods play

My doughty line was most worthily sired
Shaped, designed by a man inspired
Between frames were all his own
But sister Mallard's speed has shown
That Gresley's Walschaerts gears combining
Have left a steam hauled record shining

War came to this land with turbulent clamour
Withdrawn were classed trains with all their glamour
I turned to troopers, important freight
Which moved along as a river in spate
North or south, both sides of the border
I strove to fulfil each control order

The peace again and normal work
A thing I'd never in my mind shirk
Queen of Scots Pullman, a playboy's ploy
Was a task for my pleasure to enjoy
But changes were coming and rumour rife
Were diesels the thing to change my life

Yes, all to true, from the publics gaze
Laid aside, forgotten, to ruminate
Upon what would be my ultimate fate
Would scrap yards burner and hammer claim
Thus, bringing to end my life of fame

But no, from bread thus segregated
Came the Cameron and partners dedicated
To give lovers of my line
On showplace of my own in time
In Fife's fair Kingdom, mark you well
I'll still go on my tale to tell

This poem was written by Thornton shedmaster Tam MacKay following the
locomotive's arrival at the depot. (Peter Walker Collection)

The Grand Scottish Tour

It is a Saturday afternoon in early February 1967 and along with two of my mates, Malcolm and Derek, I am on Kirkcaldy station trainspotting and chatting. Derek says, 'Have you heard about the rail tour running at Easter? It's a grand tour of Scotland, over 600 miles in one day and it's only 30 shillings for a half fare.'

This was not something to be missed, as there was to be some steam haulage and, with steam coming to an end in May of that year, this could be the last chance. So we decided to go if at all possible.

'Did you hear that', said Malcolm, 'sounds like an A4 whistle'. 'Can't be', says I, 'the last one was withdrawn last September'. But he was right, as seconds later an A4 appeared from under Bennochy bridge and sped through the station. We thought we were seeing things, but it was real. 60009 *Union of South Africa*, which we knew had been withdrawn in the previous year, had just passed before our very eyes. What was going on?

We later found out that 60009 had been bought by a 'Fife farmer' and was out on a test run from Thornton sheds in preparation for the rail tour we had heard about. British Railways were hiring Number 9 back for the day from John Cameron, who unbeknownst to us had not only bought the locomotive but planned to run it on his farm at Lochty in the east of Fife.

We had to go on this, and so our tickets were booked. The trouble was that everyone else, or so it seemed, wanted to go too – so much so that when the train pulled into Edinburgh Waverley on Saturday 25 March, it comprised of eighteen coaches and had two Type 4 diesels at the front for the first section of the tour, down to Carlisle via Hawick and then up to Perth via Stirling, where Number 9 was to take over for the next section to Aberdeen via Forfar. Unfortunately, because of the length of the train and the mile-a-minute schedule, Number 9 was to be piloted by one of Perth shed's Black 5s, which was a bit of a disappointment.

On arrival at Perth 60009 *Union of South Africa* and 44997 were waiting and were soon coupled on.

Departure was on time, but the train was no sooner moving when it ground to a halt, to pick up two passengers who were so busy taking photographs, they failed to get on, the sympathetic guard making an emergency brake application to allow them to board.

The Stanier and Gresley combination then set off in fine style, and were soon speeding along the now closed Strathmore route towards Forfar, where the two locomotives

My ticket for the Grand Scottish tour. Fantastic value for money. (Michael Mather Collection)

2nd CLASS (269

25th March 1967

SOUVENIR TICKET

GRAND SCOTTISH TOUR

Edinburgh (Waverley) to

EDINBURGH (WAVERLEY)

AND BACK

Out via Hawick, Carlisle, Stirling, Perth

Ret. via Aberdeen, Aviemore, Larbert.

Polmont

(H) For conditions see over   Fare 30/-

On that memorable Easter Saturday in 1967, Black 5 No. 44997 and 60009 *Union of South Africa* head the eighteen-coach Grand Scottish Tour between Stonehaven and Aberdeen. (Fraser Birrell Collection)

sounded their whistles the whole length of the town. The crews were certainly playing to the gallery, and it got better, as beyond Forfar at Farnell Road, they hit 82 mph, the fastest speed on the run. This was followed by an 80 mph speed at Stonehaven, and what a spectacle this must have been as this long train passed through the station. After these high speeds, the train arrived at Aberdeen on time.

Number 9 and 44997 had hauled their massive train the 90 miles from Perth to Aberdeen in 85 minutes, a credit to the crews and the shed staff at Thornton and Perth who had prepared the locomotives.

Of course LNER and LMS rivalry came to the fore with one camp claiming it was the first time an A4 had pushed a Black 5 and hauled eighteen coaches and the other that the Black 5 had hauled the A4 and eighteen coaches. In truth, both locomotives had done well.

Two Type 2 diesels took over the train for the GNSR section from Aberdeen to Keith, then down Speyside to Aviemore, where a third Type 2 was added to get the heavy train over Drumochter on the Highland main line to Perth.

Meanwhile, Number 9 and 44997 had returned to Perth to take over the train for the final section to Edinburgh via Stirling.

Signal checks prevented any of the fireworks of earlier in the day, but they did well to top Gleneagles summit at 40 mph as 44997 was reportedly short of steam.

On arrival at Edinburgh Waverley 44997 came off the train and Number 9 took the empty stock down to Craigentinny carriage sidings. This was thought by all to be Number 9's last run with a main line train, but little did they know would happen six years later. The story had only just begun.

Michael Mather

Lochty Private Railway

Following the purchase of *Union of South Africa*, owner John Cameron was aware that steam would no longer be allowed to run on BR metals.

It was coincidental that he was in the process of purchasing Lochty farm in the East Neuk of Fife. The last section, approximately three quarters of a mile, of the East Fife Central Railway was situated on the land and was in the process of being lifted. This became the ideal solution for finding a home for his new purchase and he set about acquiring redundant colliery track and relaying this section of the line. Once the loco was delivered by road in April 1967, the lads who had volunteered their cleaning skills at Thornton again offered to prepare the loco every Sunday when it ran back and forth on the line. The youthful gang comprised myself, my own brother Davy Cant, Neil Woods, Davy Murray and Jim Kirk.

Running days were limited by work on the farm, usually from June till early September when the harvesting took place. A normal Sunday would see us arrive around 9.00 a.m. and, as the whole line including the agricultural-style shed built to house the engine was built on a gradient, would see someone dispatched to collect a tractor and chain from the farmyard down the road to pull it into the open air before lighting the fire. A water supply from the farm buildings had been laid 300 yards away in order to top up the tender. Coal was supplied by lorry in hundredweight sacks and heaved into the tender from the loading bank alongside the loco.

During the first summer of running we were not trusted to carry out any maintenance or oiling on the loco as this was the domain of some railway friends of Mr Cameron. We merely prepared the fire and completed cleaning tasks, but still felt an important part of the operation. Additionally, it was necessary to carry out continuous maintenance of the

On what was the last working along the Fife Coast line following closure in 1965, Number 9 is hauled by a Class 08 shunter as it approaches Crail, from where it will travel to Lochty by low-loader. The wagons between the locomotives are to spread the weight out, on a line that had probably never seen a Pacific before. (Ken Reid)

In the first season of operation, double-headed Fordson tractors haul Number 9 out of its shed prior to lighting the fire. (LPR)

track as it had previously only been deemed fit for colliery locos and wagons and had never carried such a heavy loco. We were tasked with walking the track each Sunday morning to check sleepers, fishplates, chairs and keys. The line climbed up through a cutting and it was also necessary to clean, repair and renew field drains in the cess throughout the season owing to the typical Scottish weather.

To enable us to ballast the line and carry heavy equipment such as jacks, we were given an addition to the motive power in the form of a blue Ford Thames van, mounted on rail wheels, along with a twin-axle wooden frame bogie. Probably a big mistake, letting us teenage lads loose with this, as we careered up and down the line all morning until the first loco movement was due! With the weight of the ballast being towed, and our antics, the rear suspension of the van soon collapsed, and the bodywork rested on the rear driving wheels. Our future trips up and down the line were accompanied by massive showers of sparks!

In the second year of running, an ex-Coronation Express observation car, originally a beaver-tail but adapted for running on the West Highland line, was purchased. This meant that we could carry passengers, so our role extended to selling and checking tickets, giving a talk to the passengers on the trip and operating the signal box that was installed for authenticity, including passing the token for single-line working. We were gradually introduced to oiling up and checking for loose nuts and bolts. How proud we were!

A further addition at Lochty was a platelayer's hut, rescued from the now closed station at St Monance. This was formed of slatted concrete panels that we dismantled

Right: Cleaning time before the visitors arrive at Lochty. Behind the smoke is Davy Murray, while Colin Cant and Neil Woods clean the boiler and Davy Cant polishes the nameplate. 1968 season. (Davy Murray)

Below: Number 9 and the observation coach depart Knightsward for Lochty in August 1970. (Michael Mather)

and rebuilt on a new concrete base just beyond the platform. A welcome shelter from the inclement Scottish weather for us. No such luck for the visitors!

Occasionally we would carry out track maintenance on a Saturday, staying overnight in the observation car. It was not unusual for some beer, whisky and homemade wine to be quaffed, and on dry evenings we would walk up a local hill to the trigpoint up top where we could identify the numerous lighthouses to be seen on the east coast of Scotland. The return journey through the fields in the dark often found us being chased by herds of curious cows.

Guard Neil Woods waves his flag to signal departure from Lochty. (Ian N. Fraser, Iain A. H. Smith Collection)

Our role as support crew gradually evolved and continued to do so throughout the period Number 9 was at Lochty. Things were beginning to change back on the main line and it soon became clear that the loco was destined for greater things, and the support crew along with it. She last ran at Lochty in 1972 and was moved by road to Ladybank on 4 April 1973 to begin the next chapter of her life.

The Lochty men came doon the glen, some like ballet dancers
One in nine had served their time, the rest were nowt but chancers.

Colin Cant

Main Line Return

On 4 April 1973 and with the 'Return to Steam' banner on the boiler casing, Number 9 leaves Lochty on a low-loader bound for Ladybank to resume her main line career, which was to last for forty-seven years. (Ian N. Fraser – Iain A. H. Smith Collection)

Having been re-railed at Ladybank, Number 9 was hauled to Kirkcaldy and is seen here with the 'Cods Mouth' open in front of the goods shed that was her home until moving to Markinch the following year. (Iain A. H. Smith Collection)

Steam returned to the main line in Scotland on 5 May 1973 on a rail tour that ran from Edinburgh to Dundee, on to Perth and Pitlochry, before returning to Edinburgh via Perth, Ladybank and Dunfermline. Steam was barred from Edinburgh at this time and so Number 9 came onto the train at Inverkeithing for the run to Dundee, where diesel took over. After turning at Dundee, Nine moved to Ladybank from where it took over the train as far as Inverkeithing. In this view it is climbing to Lochmuir summit soon after leaving Ladybank. (Michael Mather)

Number 9 stands at Dalnaspidal on the Highland main line on 2 June 1973, while a southbound passenger train passes. The locomotive was on its way to Inverness to take part in an open day, becoming the first A4 to travel over this line. (Davy Murray)

A regular event in the diary for many years was the air show at RAF Leuchars, which was held on Battle of Britain day every September. Number 9 is seen here in 1976 being hauled into the base by one of the their NBL diesel shunters. On these visits a small charge was made to visit the footplate, the money raised going to the RAF Benevolent Fund. (Davy Murray)

Number 9 crosses Invertiel viaduct, Kirkcaldy, with a train sponsored by the Kirkcaldy Lions Club. It ran from Kirkcaldy to Perth via Linlithgow and Stirling on 28 June 1977. The train included some of the SRPS' historic coaches. (Davy Murray)

Maintenance, the Trilby and Adrenalin

When Number 9 was based at Markinch shed, locomotive maintenance could be awkward as there was no pit and a platform stood adjacent to the track, but a surprising and wide variety of work happened there. Being employed at the time in a local engineering company had its advantages, with access to a wide range of machine tools where parts could readily be manufactured or repaired.

During 1977, after dismantling the tender brake rigging, it became apparent that a complete set of new bushes and pins would be necessary, and I was asked if these could be made at work. There was a lot of material and machining hours required so a price was agreed with my gaffer. Sketches were made, material cut and machined complete, then came a hand-written invoice for cash payment. A few weeks later I took the money to the gaffer and, you've probably guessed it, I'm certain the envelope went straight in his back pocket! Never mind, a lot of that type of thing happened then. 'Homers' were commonplace, and the new parts were undeniably a bargain.

Most jobs were done on the quiet and easier to conceal from the foremen. They were machined during night shift breaks and usually over a couple of consecutive nights. Others were not so easy to keep hidden and during a boiler re-tube, the dome cover was found to need face skimming. I didn't have a car then and relied on a lift to get to work and had some explaining to do one particular night. The driver wasn't best pleased when asked to put a large A4 dome cover in the boot of his brand-new Austin Maxi, but kindly

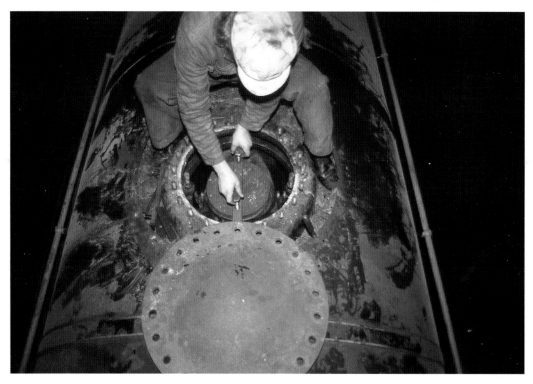

Graeme works on the regulator valve while the dome cover that weighed down the Austin Maxi can be seen at photographer Davy's feet. (Davy Murray)

obliged anyway. My workbag was frequently weighed down with A4 parts going in or coming out of work, including fitted bolts, studs, pins, bushes and gland packings to name a few. Gatehouse security must have occasionally wondered why I walked so stooped while carrying my bag; or more likely, they simply turned a blind eye.

When the A4 and K4 were at Thornton shed, we thought it beneficial to have some machinery to manufacture or repair parts on-site. I was then a workshop lecturer at a local college and knew that an older lathe was due for disposal. After inquiring how much it was going for, the response was 'scrap value'. I made a quite ridiculous offer, which was most surprisingly accepted. The lathe, a good condition Dean, Smith & Grace, was installed at the shed and was well used during its time there. However, when it became apparent that DB Schenker wanted the site cleared for forthcoming demolition, the machine had to be sold and a buyer found quickly. To cut a long story short, it was sold to LNWR Heritage, who got a good machine for a very fair price indeed. The funny thing is though, I was really fortunate in receiving ten times the amount that was originally paid!

Travelling on the locomotive is a truly remarkable experience and I want to share a condensed version of my first main line run. In 1978 on an Edinburgh–Stirling–Perth and return charter, I was on the footplate for the return leg. I have to say, I felt a strange mix of excitement and apprehension. We departed Perth on time and soon started climbing towards Moncrieff tunnel. The traction inspector, complete with dust coat and trilby, stood behind the driver, the fireman was feeding the incandescent fire, and I was standing behind his seat looking forward to a good run, especially after joining the fast Edinburgh–Glasgow line at Polmont. As we approached the tunnel the three-cylinder exhaust beat was clear and crisp as we powered on and just before entering the tunnel the safety valves lifted! The noise was ear shattering as we entered the tunnel and debris from the tunnel roof was being blown back into the cab through the roof vents. When we came out the other side into the fading daylight, everyone was covered in grime and I started to wonder just what I'd let myself in for. Heading south from Hilton Junction, Number 9 picked up the pace and accelerated towards Auchterarder, through Gleneagles and on towards Dunblane.

As we passed Dunblane station, the traction inspector turned grinning, and shouted 'hold on to something son', but did not say why. I thought there may be a slight kink in the track ahead and ignored his advice thinking I'll be fine! Number 9 darted into Kippenross tunnel and about halfway through there was a violent lurch and an almighty bang. I nearly jumped clean out of my skin and only just managed to regain my composure before clearing the tunnel. I looked over and caught the crew smirking; they were visibly amused and knew the young lad would get a bit of a fright on such a bad bit of track. Nevertheless, I was getting into this and totally enjoying the experience by then.

On the busy E&G main line I was eager to have a fast run and wasn't disappointed. We needed to maintain our path between service trains and not be hindered by adverse signals. In the darkness the cab was illuminated by the white-hot fire; the driver had the regulator fully opened and was quickly accelerating the train. Number 9's exhaust beat was syncopated as speed rose to over 70 mph and we charged on relentlessly into the darkness of the night. At one point the driver glanced over his shoulder to the traction inspector, who was firmly holding onto his trilby! The inspector merely looked away and said nothing – the speedometer was reading just under 90 mph! All signals were

Locomotive
Inspector Jimmy
Adams in
regulation trilby
looks down from
the footplate to
driver Tommy
Farrell and
John Cameron
at Kirkcaldy
in April 1973.
(Davy Murray)

showing green and we had the most amazing high-speed run before having to slow. Arrival at Edinburgh Waverley was somewhat early as we eased to a halt at platform 19. In no time at all, many of the passengers rushed out of the coaches and thronged around the locomotive to voice their appreciation for such a good run and to shake hands with the crew.

Even after all these years, that particular trip was the most incredible, adrenalin-charged and extraordinary experience I'll never forget.

Gordon McHattie

Markinch Works

 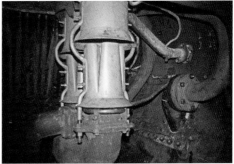

Above left: Markinch Goods Shed, or 'Markinch Works' as Ian called it, could be a hive of activity, not only with routine maintenance, but also quite major work on the locomotive. Front bogie removal, the fitting of new piston valve liners, the lowering of the boiler casing and a boiler re-tube were just some of the jobs tackled. Here, the superheater elements are being fitted to the header following the re-tube in May 1980. (Davy Murray)

Above right: With the re-tube complete and all steam pipes fitted, the last thing to be done was the fitting of the shiny new Kylchap exhaust cowls. (Davy Murray)

Towards the end of the re-tube work, Number 9 awaits the fitting of the Bugatti nose. (Davy Murray)

Left: Wee Graeme with the big drill. Behind are Herbert (nearest) and Lindsay. Herbert Ward, who sadly passed away shortly after Lindsay, was a retired paper mill engineer and a skilled turner. He would often knock up parts for Nine on the lathe he had in his garden shed. (Ian Leven)

Below: Winter maintenance 1983 and the locomotive has been split from the tender to have work done on the tender drawbars and the loco brakes. (Ian Leven)

What's That Smell?

An Easter trip from Edinburgh to Aberdeen was a regular feature of Number 9's main line programme for many years during the 1970s and 1980s, and 1981 was to be no different with Number 9 scheduled to haul the Strathdon Express on 18 April. The tour, as always, was organised by the Scottish Steam Railtours Group.

Unusually, the route was from Edinburgh via Stirling and Perth to Dundee rather than the Fife route crossing the Forth and Tay bridges. And so we set off from Edinburgh along the E&G, in superb weather that was to last all day.

Everything was going fine until north of Stonehaven it became apparent to those on the footplate that something was wrong. A strong smell that was at first thought to be crop spraying was soon realised to be coming from the engine. The aniseed stink bomb that is fitted to the centre big end to warn of overheating must have burst.

The train was brought to a halt at Newtonhill signal box, 10 miles short of Aberdeen, and wee Graeme was sent under the engine to have a look. He came back with the bad news that not only had the big end brass overheated, but it had also disintegrated and there was only a small part left. Help was summoned from Ferryhill shed at Aberdeen and a Class 47 soon arrived to rescue the train while Number 9 was shunted into a siding for further examination.

The driver being experienced on A4s from driving them in the sixties reckoned that he could get Number 9 to Ferryhill shed without causing any more damage, and so, with much clanking and at a very slow pace, Number 9 made its way to Ferryhill.

Once on shed and over a pit Lindsay, Davie and Graeme soon had the centre connecting rod removed and emerged from under the loco with the good news that the big end journal had survived and could be made serviceable. It was now a race against time, as Number 9 was booked to take over the North Briton rail tour at Mossend on 9 May.

The undamaged centre big end journal after removal of the connecting rod at Ferryhill Shed. (Davy Murray)

Half of the new big end brass already white-metalled. (Davy Murray)

What followed was a superb piece of co-operation between ourselves; the Ferryhill fitters; John Graham of the A4 Locomotive Society, who provided drawings for the new big end brass; Robert Ferlie Iron Founders of Auchtermuchty, whose subsidiaries Fife Pattern Makers and St John's Foundry made a new pattern and cast the new brass bush; and finally their engineers who travelled to Aberdeen to take measurements before carrying out the machining and white-metalling of the bush.

It was touch and go as to whether Number 9 would be ready or not, but all came right in the end. It made its way to Mossend, the big end getting run in on the way, and took over the North Briton as scheduled.

The route of this tour was from Mossend to Dundee via Stirling and Perth.

The return trip to Larbert via the Tay and Forth bridges was to be the last steam trip for the driver, who was due to retire and intended to go out on a high, not sparing the horses as he sped through Fife. I remember Lindsay saying 'a thought we wur going to go up the platform at Cupar!' I, meanwhile, was standing at Ladybank station with my wife and sister-in-law as Nine came flying round the curve and away through the station, my sister-in-law commenting 'If they were as fast as that, why did they stop using them?' Says it all really.

Michael Mather

The 1980s

Number 9's first trip after the 1980 boiler re-tube was to Aviemore with a short private special train, The Royal Highlander, on 27 June. It was conveying, among others, Lord Mansfield of Scone Palace. It continued on to Inverness, light engine to turn. This was a trial run for an Edinburgh to Inverness special in August of that year. This view was taken during a stop at Newtonmore. (Ian Leven)

John Cameron is at the regulator as Number 9 starts the descent from Lochmuir summit to Ladybank with a Severn Valley Railway-sponsored tour on 29 November 1980. The train had started in Birmingham, with Number 9 taking over at Edinburgh for the run to Dundee where there was still a turntable. The return run to Edinburgh was via Perth and Stirling. (Davy Murray)

Left: John Cameron proudly poses in front of his locomotive at Aberdeen on 30 May 1981. The occasion was to celebrate the inauguration of the Flying Scotsman service running from Aberdeen to London Kings Cross powered by the InterCity 125. (Davy Murray)

Below: Number 9 first ventured south of the border in preservation in 1984 to work a number of Cumbrian Mountain Express and Scarborough Spa Express services during April and May of that year. It is seen here at Carnforth with the support crew and Elizabethan headboard. From left: Davy, Fraser, Lindsay, Gary, Graeme, Ian and Chris. (Fraser Birrell Collection)

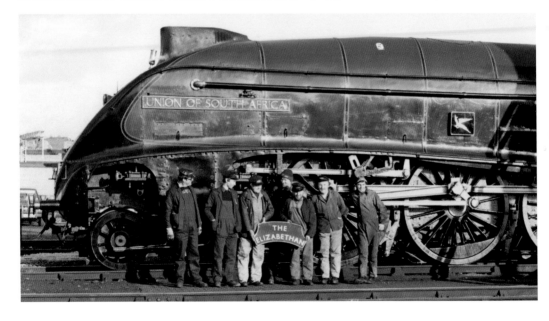

Game for a Laugh

In the autumn of 1985 Number 9 was due to haul a series of trains from London Marylebone to Stratford-upon-Avon.

On 14 September, Nine hauled an SRPS special from Kilmarnock to Keighley. Having travelled engine and coach, we had a borrowed coach for this trip, from Markinch to Ayr the previous day. Nine then continued on to York where it was due to lay over before continuing to London.

Unfortunately, following an inspection a broken driving axle spring was discovered. This fault alone, which was soon repaired, shouldn't have prevented the onward journey to the capital, but a series of petty politics that followed meant that the whole trip was aborted, much to the displeasure of the support crew, especially Lindsay, who had commemorative T-shirts made for the event.

Number 9 therefore remained at York until its planned return to Scotland, hauling a northbound Cumbrian Mountain Express as far as Carlisle on 30 November.

The day of the trip dawned damp and dreich, a big change from the extremely hard frost of the previous evening when any water dripping from the engine was freezing.

The trip to Carlisle was fairly uneventful, water being taken at Long Preston followed by a good climb of the Long Drag to Ribblehead and a photo stop at Garsdale before passing Aisgill summit. On arrival at Carlisle, Number 9 came off and took water while the National Railway Museum's pioneer EE Type 4 (Class 40) D200 coupled on to take the train back south.

This was where the fun began, as we were now booked to move to Annan, from where a diesel, that was supposedly on its way from Glasgow to meet us, was to pilot us to Glasgow Eastfield shed, where we would spend the night before returning to Markinch. Unfortunately, on arrival at Annan we found out that the diesel, a Class 37, had only just left Glasgow and it would be a couple of hours before it arrived. The driver, fireman and traction inspector soon departed, as it was the end of their shift, and so we were left to our own devices.

We now had a big problem as the tender was low on coal and although there was enough to keep Nine in steam until the diesel arrived, there wouldn't now be enough to get us to Glasgow, steam still being required, even though Nine was being hauled by a diesel, to lubricate the cylinders.

As it happened we were parked right next to a coal yard adjacent to Annan signal box, and so Lindsay went up to the signalman to explain our predicament and to ask if he could contact the coalman to see if we could buy a ton of coal. The coalman, on answering the phone, thought it was a wind-up, even thinking that it was *Game for a Laugh*, a popular TV program of the time, which played practical jokes on members of the public. It took some persuading from the signalman that there was indeed a steam locomotive in need of coal.

Eventually the coalman was persuaded and came out to help us, filling bags of coal that we then hauled up the side of the tender. Of course, sod's law had now entered this pantomime and the rain that had been light and on and off since we arrived at Annan started to pour down, which really added to the fun of hauling the bags up! The job was eventually done and with the instruction to 'send the bill to Mr Cameron' the coalman made his way home.

It is evening at Annan and the camera flash has bounced off the light rain that is falling, as Fraser and fireman Gordon Hodgson look down from the cab. Gordon, a true gentleman and a pleasure to work with, had started his railway career at the former North British and LNER Carlisle Canal shed, so knew all about Gresley engines. (Michael Mather)

Our work wasn't over yet though, as when the diesel arrived only a driver was provided for Number 9, so we took it in turns to fire. This was the first time I had fired on the main line, and to be honest I wasn't very good, missing the firehole on occasion – much to the amusement of the driver.

Eventually we reached Eastfield, and were glad. It had been a long day, but at least we got a long lie-in on the Sunday as the return to Markinch wasn't until the afternoon.

And so ended what should have been a triumphant return from London. But never mind, nine years later we would really make the headlines in the capital.

Michael Mather

Overhaul Against the Clock

I had been absent from Markinch shed for some weeks towards the end of 1988 due to a family bereavement, but one Monday night in January 1989 I made my way down to the shed to see what was happening – nothing much had occurred since Number 9's boiler certificate expired in 1987.

Approaching the shed I could hear work going on, and on entering I was greeted by 'Are we glad to see you' from Lindsay and Davy. They went on to explain that Number 9 was required to work specials in connection with the Forth Bridge centenary commencing in March 1990, and was to travel to Bridgnorth on the Severn Valley Railway for a major overhaul, so it was all hands on deck to get Nine ready for its journey south.

This would be its first major overhaul since leaving Doncaster works in 1963, Nine being the last A4 to be overhauled there.

Number 9 left Markinch diesel-hauled on 22 February and, after a brief visit to Thornton shed where it was put over the pit for examination, started its journey south before arriving at Bridgnorth on 24 February. Dismantling work started straight away, with some of the support crew travelling down to help with this.

The engineers at 'The Valley' were up against time for this work, which would have to be completed by the end of the year to enable Nine to be run in and main line tested before its big day on the 4 March 1990, the centenary of the opening of the Forth Bridge. An overhaul of this magnitude had never been attempted in such a short time

Work stripping down Number 9 started immediately on arrival at the Severn Valley. Taking a break and posing for the camera are, top from left: Lindsay, Davy and Ian. Bottom: SVR engineers Mike Heitzman and Roy Mort, and Fraser. (Support Crew Collection)

The boiler sits in Bridgnorth yard following removal from the frames. The boiler was built in 1960 and first fitted to 60023 *Golden Eagle* before being fitted to Nine as part of the 1963 overhaul – its thirteenth boiler change. (Davy Murray)

Seen on the other side of the yard are a collection of A4 parts including the cab, blastpipe and superheater tubes. (Davy Murray)

With all the wheels removed, the frames and running plate stand in the shed at Bridgnorth. (Davy Murray)

in the preservation era, so it was fingers crossed that they made it. The work, apart from the boiler and mechanicals, would include a new ash pan and a complete rebuild of the tender from the chassis up, the water tank being in poor condition.

We weren't going to be idle at Markinch over the coming year either. Mr Cameron had acquired a support coach for us, and so 1989 was spent rubbing it down in preparation for repainting in BR maroon and the conversion of the parcels space into a workshop and a kitchen.

Work on Number 9 progressed rapidly during 1989 and by 15 December the boiler was ready for a steam test, observed by BR boiler inspector Sam Foster. The test was successful and the boiler was lifted onto the frames four days later. This allowed final assembly to be completed and Number 9 made its first run under its own steam on 30 January.

Running in on 'The Valley' commenced immediately, sixteen return trips being run before Nine left for Derby and its main line test run on 22 February. The test route was from Derby to Sheffield and return.

The test run being a success, Number 9 headed for Carlisle with a Severn Valley support crew in readiness to work the southbound Citadel Express over the Settle to Carlisle Railway. Unfortunately, trouble was to strike at Shipley when a Cartazzi bearing started to overheat. Fortunately the Worth Valley Railway was nearby, and Nine was put in there for repairs and running in of the replacement bearing before continuing on to Carlisle, which was reached on Saturday 24 February – just in time for its booked working south. This was where we joined the Severn Valley support crew, having travelled down by road to Carlisle Upperby.

Running without nameplates for the first time, Number 9 and the Ethel train heating locomotive draw away from Carlisle Upperby shed prior to working the Citadel Express. (Davy Murray)

In the strong wind, Ian holds onto his hat while keeping an eye on the tender water level at the Garsdale water stop that was to prove so costly. (Davy Murray)

This was a day of heavy rain and high winds, but Number 9 put in a brilliant performance on the climb to Aisgill with its heavy train, which included an Ethel train heating locomotive, topping the summit at 40 mph.

Little did we know during the water stop at Garsdale the trouble the high acidic water would cause, as by the time we got to Haworth on the Worth Valley Railway, having turned on the Shipley triangle, a major leak of the back lap joint in the firebox had occurred, meaning Nine wouldn't be able to work its planned northbound trip to Carlisle the following day.

Boilersmiths from 'The Valley' were summoned and the following day's train was changed to diesel northbound with 3442 *The Great Marquess*, which was at Carlisle Upperby depot, hauling the train south. Nick and I were volunteered to travel to Carlisle on the train to assist the SVR support crew.

Firebox repairs carried out, Number 9 finally left Haworth on Friday 2 March, two days before the centenary special. It made its way to Thornton, which was to be its new home, before heading over to Edinburgh on the Saturday for the big day on 4 March. Phew, that was close!

Michael Mather

Bird of Prey

With the upcoming Forth Bridge centenary celebrations and Number 9's high-profile involvement, it was felt that its name, being very loosely associated with the Republic of South Africa and its apartheid regime, would not look good during what would be national and worldwide coverage of the event.

In truth the name *Union of South Africa* had nothing to do with the South Africa of 1990, but there was ignorance among a minority of the general public who would connect the two and may cause trouble. Hints of this had already happened when Number 9 was to haul a number of specials in connection with the Edinburgh festival a few years earlier.

Luckily, rather than run nameless, there was an alternative. When Number 9 was built in 1937, it was allocated the name *Osprey*, continuing on the bird theme from A4s *Golden Eagle* and *Kingfisher*, built in 1936, and *Falcon*, built in 1937. The *Osprey* nameplates were never fitted, the name going instead to A4 4494.

The *Osprey* name was a very fitting one for a Scotland-based locomotive as the bird, which is making a comeback from near extinction, is very much associated with Scotland.

And so the decision was taken, and new nameplates were cast and were fitted at Edinburgh Waverley station on the eve of the Forth Bridge centenary.

Number 9 carried the *Osprey* name until the autumn of 1991 when the 'big plates' were refitted, the *Union of South Africa* name being unveiled by BR's InterCity director Dr John Prideaux at a ceremony in Edinburgh Waverley station on 15 September.

Michael Mather

It is after midnight on the eve of the Forth Bridge centenary, and Waverley station is closed for the night as Ian, Graeme, Lindsay and Nick fit the new *Osprey* nameplate to the driver's side. All day we had been questioned about what name the loco would be carrying, but we didn't disclose anything and kept everybody waiting until the big day. (Michael Mather)

The Forth Bridge Centenary

60009 *Osprey* proudly stands at Edinburgh Waverley ready to depart for the Forth Bridge and the centenary celebrations on 4 March 1990, with the centenary ceremony taking place on the bridge itself. A flat wagon on the up side was used for this purpose. (Davy Murray)

Above left: At the end of a busy day, Nine had hauled the centenary special to the bridge and return, and then in the afternoon a special to Perth and return, so it was now time to head back to Thornton. Crossing the bridge there was a searchlight on the shore that tracked us across the bridge, a very memorable moment and one that was captured by the television cameras. (Davy Murray)

Above right: The support crew were all presented with a centenary badge and tie. (Michael Mather Collection)

Davy Murray loved to take night shots and this one shows Number Nine at Thornton yard, her home from 1990 to 1992 before returning to Markinch. As well as the centenary celebrations during March and April of 1990, Nine was used by ScotRail to train four new steam drivers to replace those that had retired. In this view it is coupled to the coaches that were used for these training runs that went round the Fife Circle and up to Perth. (Davy Murray)

From March to October 1990, Number 9 worked a number of Forth centenary specials from Edinburgh to Perth via the Forth Bridge and Fife, returning via Stirling. Here, with the head of the Dutch railways hanging out the cab, Nine climbs from Markinch to Lochmuir summit on 2 September. (Jules Hathaway)

I Don't Think They Are Coming Back for You

In September 1990 60009 was tasked to move from Carnforth up to Skipton then on to Appleby over the Settle to Carlisle line. At that time Carnforth was open to the public and a family of four showed up late afternoon. We showed the daughter and her father around the loco. After the visit we said farewell to the family, and they said they may see us the following day.

The following day we had a late departure from Carnforth at about 10.00 a.m. (normally we have an early start of between 4.00 a.m. and 6.00 a.m.). The journey was uneventful, and we arrived in Skipton in plenty of time prior to the train arriving from York. I was nominated to do the souvenir trolley. I changed out of overalls back into trousers and shirt.

The train loco detached and 60009 with support coach reversed onto the train. I made my way to the back of the train and started my sales pitch. The engine sounded good as I wended my way through the train.

Our first stop was to take water at Garsdale and then we carried on to Appleby, from where the *Duchess of Hamilton* was to return the train back to York. As the passengers had alighted, 60009 pulled the train into the siding to the rear of signal box. The *Duchess*, with support coach, then attached to the rear of the train.

On a day I was very much on the train. I'm sitting in the fireman's seat as Number 9 approaches Aisgill summit at the head of The Streamline Express on 16 November 1991, having just broken the record for the climb from Appleby. With a reduced load of eight coaches due to leaf fall, Nine had covered the 15.25 miles in nineteen minutes forty-five seconds and topped the summit at 59 mph. (Peter Drummond)

Another view on the Settle to Carlisle line, from 30 March 2002, as Nine climbs the long drag from Settle to Ribblehead. (Davy Murray)

While all this was on going, I had left the train and decided to photograph the *Duchess* and possibly *Union of South Africa*. I met up with the family whom we had seen at Carnforth the previous day. The eldest girl was excited to see two steam engines and we stood on the bridge as the *Duchess* moved out of the siding and into the platform. After the departure of the *Duchess*, Number 9 reversed out of the siding and backed down the up platform and at this point I walked down to meet the support coach. I then started to run but one of the other crew told me not to worry, the loco was only going to take water at the dairy. I then joined the family on the bridge again. I was expecting the loco to move up to the signal box and cross over to the down line and reverse back to the dairy, which stands to the south of Appleby station.

When the loco crossed over to the down line it then proceeded to climb away towards Carlisle. The girl then said, 'John, I don't think the train is coming back'. Sadly, I stood on the station bridge watching the A4 and support coach disappear. My thoughts then turned to how one gets back to the support coach. Lucky for me I had enough money and a rail card in my pocket to enable me to get back to Carlisle.

On arrival in Carlisle station, I headed for the information desk. My question to the staff was about where the steam locos stable overnight. I was told 'Oh they are at Kingmoor'. Not knowing any better, I then found a bus to take me all the way to Kingmoor. I arrived only to find Kingmoor was closed years before. Back to Carlisle railway station I went and looked for a pall of smoke. There was a lot of smoke visible off to the south of the station, so I made my way towards it.

To my amazement I found Number 9 at Upperby and all the lads were wondering what had happened to me. In those days there were no mobile phones. After this incident it is usual, before departure, for the crew to ask, 'Is John Lynch on the train?'

John Lynch

What's in a Name?

It is April 1991 and we are in Crewe for a stint of running on the North Wales coast line to Holyhead for a few weeks. It is early evening and we are walking out for our evening meal at The Cheshire Casserole restaurant. The banter is lively, even before we've had a drink. Lindsay tells us we have been offered more trips in August and September in place of 60007 *Sir Nigel Gresley*, which will not be ready in time. Lindsay said 'it would be funny if we borrowed No. 7's plates and ran as Gresley'. I replied that 'they would get all the credit and not us'. Davy thought out loud about long-scrapped sister locos.

We came up initially with 60029 *Woodcock*, as we would only have to change one cab-side number. That was quickly dismissed as it was not a Haymarket engine and the length of nameplate would mean cutting more holes in the boiler casing to mount the nameplate. What was a Haymarket engine with a six-letter name? 'MERLIN', shouted Nick, '60027'. 'That would work' said Lindsay. And so a plan started to form!

We talked more over the meal and drinks and it was agreed that NO ONE would know anything about it. Secrecy was the key word.

The political world was becoming more tolerant of South Africa and John Cameron was ready to put the big plates, the original name, back on, so now was the perfect time. Lindsay spoke with John and he agreed to the idea. Davy organised the nameplates with

With the nameplates fitted, the support and loco crew pose beside *Merlin*. From left: Davy, John and Lindsay, Inspector Bill Andrews, Dick Hardy, and the loco crew. Former Stratford and Stewarts Lane shedmaster Dick Hardy was always a welcome guest in the support coach, arriving as he did with one of his many photograph albums and a Battenburg cake! He would always work his passage too, taking a wee turn on the shovel. (Support Crew Collection, with thanks to Dick Hardy)

his cousin David Murray of Cine-Rail video fame. David had the nameplates cast in solid brass at a foundry in Leeds and the number plate made there too. Four nameplates were cast as Lindsay, myself, Johnnie and John Cameron wanted one. Nick set about making a replica ships crest of HMS *Merlin*, which the loco carried on the driver's side midway along the boiler. I took on the job of making the cab-side transfers.

We had enough Brunswick green and black paint in the shed, but I needed the beige for the numbers. I went to Beattie's toy shop in Perth to get some Humbrol paint. 'Can I help you'? asked the assistant. 'I need some paint as I'm renumbering a steam loco' I told him. 'What gauge is it, double O'? he enquired. 'Err no, 12 inches to the foot!' was my reply, which somewhat surprised him. I found an appropriate colour, which he agreed should be right and I paid for it and left. I made two sets so if one got damaged being applied there was a replacement. In time all was set and everything was in place safely in the support coach. August came and Number 9 headed for Crewe.

After a couple of weeks of running to Holyhead and back all was well with the loco, but one crew did have a rough trip one day. And then something happened. On the Wednesday between the runs to Holyhead a man walked into the Crewe Heritage Centre and started a conversation with Lindsay. After a few minutes he said, 'Is there any truth in the rumour you're going to run as Merlin for a month?' Lindsay spat his tea out in surprise and asked, 'Where the hell did you hear that?' The man went on to say he had been in a foundry in Leeds and saw the nameplates during the casting process. He put two and two together and actually came up with four! Lindsay composed himself

Looking superb and with Lindsay at the regulator, *Merlin* moves down the yard at the Crewe Heritage Centre. (Davy Murray)

and took the man into the coach and showed him the nameplates and begged him to keep it a secret. He offered Lindsay £400 for one of the plates, which Lindsay turned down as they were all spoken for.

Also at Crewe was A3 4472 *Flying Scotsman*, but it was a little poorly. It was booked for a Sunday trip down the Welsh Marches but had failed, so we were offered the tour. It was decided THIS would be the time to unveil the surprise. So, having come back from the evening meal the guys set about renaming and renumbering the loco. Under the cover of darkness 60009 *Osprey* became 60027 *Merlin*. In the pre-Internet days, the short-notice replacement was not known about, so the passengers and lineside photographers were expecting the A3 NOT an A4.

Everyone was stunned. Where did this loco come from and what happened to Number 9? During the day the telephone at the Crewe Heritage Centre was red hot and Tony Moseley was kept very busy. Having taken the umpteenth call asking, where did 60027 come from? His answer became 'the strategic reserve!'. The strategic reserve is a mythological collection of steam locos kept in a secret location ready to come out and save the nation in time of railway crisis. Some European countries actually did have one, but not the UK. So, 60027 sets off merrily on its way to Shrewsbury, which was as far as it was allowed on this occasion, leaving a trail of disbelief in its wake. We heard later that one photographer did not manage a photograph as he stood mouth agog watching it go by and not believing what he was seeing.

The loco ran as 60027 *Merlin* for the rest of its stay in Crewe and the light engine run back to Fife. The loco inspector who had the bad trip early on had a second trip with a different crew and commented in all seriousness that this loco was better than the one he was on last time. The overall response was overwhelming and the renaming was a great success, the railway press having a field day. InterCity steam boss David Ward claimed when asked about it, that it was a light-hearted request from himself. Cheeky ****** knew nothing about it.

Back in Fife at the end of September and 60027 briefly became on one cab-side only 60029 and then back to 60009. Also, the big plates were put back on and a special train was organised to run from Edinburgh Waverley to Perth after the loco had its *Union of South Africa* name revealed by Dr John Prideaux, chairman of BR InterCity.

Nick made a beautiful job of the *HMS Merlin* badge. It was held on by a hook round the vacuum ejector pipe and a magnet on the back of the badge secured it to the boiler casing. (Davy Murray)

60027 Merlin at the head of The Welsh Marches Express leaves Chester on its way to Shrewsbury on 31 August 1991, the day everyone at the lineside thought they were seeing things. (David Hunt)

The last word on what we called the *Merlin* affair must belong to our dear late chief engineer Lindsay. We were at Waverley before the unveiling and David Ward came up to Lindsay and said, 'I hope you didn't get into too much trouble from John [Cameron] over the *Merlin* renaming.' Lindsay just looked at him and replied, 'Mr Ward, we don't do ANYTHING without Mr Cameron's permission,' then turned and walked away from him.

In February 1992 we were to work a special train to celebrate the 150th anniversary of the Edinburgh & Glasgow Railway, the E&G. Guest of honour was Lord William Whitelaw, whose grandfather, also William Whitelaw, was a director of the LNER. For this trip we officially renamed and renumbered the loco 60004 *William Whitelaw* in honour of Lord Whitelaw's grandfather.

Jules Hathaway

Name Dropping

In the first week of November of 1992 Aberdeen celebrated the 125th anniversary of the joint station and a week of events was planned. Number 9 was to be there for the week to be in steam in the station and available for visits to the footplate with a short special train to Inverurie and back on the Wednesday of the week. On Sunday 1 November 60009 and the support coach left Thornton for the run to Aberdeen, which went without incident. On arrival we turned on the turntable at the site of Ferryhill depot, a one-time home shed of 60009, and then made ourselves comfortable in the yard to the rear of the station. Most of the support crew went home and Colin and I settled in for the week.

Every morning Inspector Lachie Duncan would arrive and move the loco into bay platform four so we could be admired by the masses. Colin and I had a great many visitors with some of the best questions asked by children.

Wednesday 4 November was the actual anniversary date and the station was buzzing with people. We had an unofficial visitor to the support coach when radio personality Robin Galloway climbed on board looking for John Cameron. I gave him a telling off for walking across several sidings in what was then still an active freight yard and told him he should not be in the coach. I told him Mr Cameron was not here yet and with that he left. I was interviewed for the radio by another presenter later in the day. The loco also did a short return special working to Inverurie station 17 miles away, where we were met by a group of local schoolchildren who had visited us on the previous Monday.

The rest of the week passed pleasantly with a trip to another part of the yard to be loaded with coal on the Thursday afternoon. Being in steam for the week meant we had to keep feeding the fire and we had a tour south to take on Sunday 8 November. Unfortunately, I didn't load as much coal as I should've done on the Thursday, which would come to back to bite us on the Sunday.

The tour south was one-way for us, and we came onto the front of the train with Number 9 proudly wearing a wreath of poppies, for this day was Remembrance Sunday. The coal situation was a tad worrying but off we set. The actual run went well but as we were passing Thornton shed the fireman returned from the coal space in the tender having swept it out. We got to Inverkeithing alright, where we came off the train as planned, but the boiler pressure was well down, and we needed something to burn to get us back to Thornton.

Inspector Lachie Duncan arranged for us to go into the yard at Inverkeithing for us to try and source some wood and sleepers. The nightwatchman was very surprised to get a visitor as John Cameron entered the bothy to say he wanted sleepers. The elderly watchman refused even when Mr Cameron offered to pay for them. Also, in the early 1990s, Mr Cameron was the chairman of ScotRail, and he was at pains to point this out to the watchman. 'I don't believe you,' he kept saying to Mr Cameron, 'If you are the chairman of ScotRail then I'm the bloody Pope!'

We did get some wood and sleepers in the end and left Inverkeithing for Thornton with a sleeper rammed into the fire-hole door, too long to go all the way in. As we made our way along the branch, the residents of Cowdenbeath and Lochgelly could have been forgiven for thinking that it was bonfire night again by the amount of sparks that were being thrown high into the air from Nine's lum. We finally reached Thornton, and so ended another exciting day in the lives of the support crew.

Now back as *Union of South Africa* and with the poppy wreath on the top lamp bracket, Number 9 is prepared for its eventful trip south from Aberdeen on 8 November 1992. (Jules Hathaway)

About eight weeks later Mr Cameron attended a presentation evening for a group of ScotRail staff who were retiring and he was presenting them with their gift. One staff member was a certain watchman from Inverkeithing and, as he approached, Mr Cameron recognised him and offered his hand and said in his booming voice 'Well how is the Pope this evening.'

Jules Hathaway

Loco Crews

Perth Locomotive Inspector Peter Annandale, 'The Prince of Darkness (don't ask), is at the regulator and keeping a close eye from behind is driver Bert Abercrombie of Thornton depot. Bert, or Aber as he was called, was a regular driver of Number 9 in the 1990s along with Thornton fireman Pete Hutton. (Support Crew Collection)

Fireman Pete Hutton and locomotive inspector Geordie Steele look down from the cab during a stop at Montrose on 1 November 1992. Pete became a driver at the 1990 crew training, but much preferred firing. (Jules Hathaway)

Sitting in his familiar seat and probably reaching for the whistle handle, John Cameron smiles for the camera. (Support Crew Collection)

Not loco crew, but vital to the running of the locomotive. British Railways mechanical inspector Brian Penny and boiler inspector Sam Foster pose for the camera while giving Number 9 its annual exam on 29 September 1993. Sam once said that 'the boiler was so good, it could make steam burning wet bus tickets!' (Jules Hathaway)

Lindsay Spittal – Chief Engineer

October 1973 saw 60009 *Union of South Africa* towed by diesel from its home in the shed beside Kirkcaldy station to the shed beside Markinch station. One new volunteer who offered his services was Lindsay Spittal. He lived across the road from the shed, was a paper mill engineer by trade and worked shifts, so he was available during the day midweek – all attributes ideally suited to the work that was to be undertaken to the engine. All the small tubes were replaced in the boiler and, unheard of now, this work was done by the support crew with outside engineers giving assistance.

Lindsay was a man 'o pairts'. A husband, father, engineer, accordion player, and lover of all things Scottish – especially whisky and good times.

He was a natural leader and quickly gained the respect and confidence of the support crew and Mr Cameron. He worked hard and played hard and expected everyone to do the same. He did tell useless volunteers to 'go away' if they were becoming a nuisance, but also encouraged anyone with an interest in steam, especially youngsters.

He oversaw too many main line trips and repairs to the engine in his twenty years to mention in detail. He was great at coordinating work between the shed and the various engineering works involved.

Main line trips always had to allow the support crew out for a meal and a few drams no matter how hard the preparatory work had been during the day. He was chief engineer through 33,292 miles of main line service. His sudden death in 1993 was a blow to everyone who knew him.

The engine's close-knit and efficient support crew is his testimony. He is remembered with affection and laughter.

Ian and Marilyn Leven

Lindsay Spittal, sadly missed.
(Support Crew Collection)

A Seat with a View

Appleby is a wonderful station on the famous Settle to Carlisle line. It is a time warp with Midland Railway-style fencing, semaphore signals and a working water crane and water tower. The S&C is probably the most popular route for steam-hauled specials in either direction. To aid the watering of steam locos in the southbound direction a water crane was reinstalled. The actual crane had somehow survived since the end of steam in 1968 and had stood at the end of the northbound platform at Lazonby station north of Appleby. In 1991 it was decided it would be removed and reinstated at Appleby to speed up the watering of southbound steam locos. The local round table raised the money for it and to rebuild the brick water tower and water tank that would feed the crane.

In May of 1993 we worked a southbound tour over the Settle to Carlisle and were booked for a photo stop and to take water at Appleby. After we had watered and pulled coal forward and the passengers were busy with their cameras, we sat on the gravel under the white stone APPLEBY name, soaking up the sun. Lindsay looked about and said, 'What this place needs is a seat for support crews to rest their weary arses!' We all agreed it would be nice to be able to sit properly and not on the ground.

Four months later the unthinkable happened. Lindsay and a few of his mates were in Aberdeen having returned from a golfing weekend on the Shetland Islands; they were off the ferry and in a pub waiting for the train home. Lindsay had a very sudden heart attack and passed away just as he always said he would... with a whisky in his hand. Everyone associated with Number 9 was totally devastated at this sudden and terrible loss.

As a group we decided we had to do something to always remember him by. Then Nick remembered what he said at Appleby a few months previously. Right, that was it – we would see about getting a seat by the water crane so 'support crews could rest their weary arses'. We set about raising money between us and others within the main line steam movement. Members of the A4 Steam Loco Preservation Society, who own and operate 4498 (as it was then) *Sir Nigel Gresley*, also had a collection as many of them knew Lindsay well too. This was generously matched by the society itself and we soon had a handsome sum. I took on the task of building the seat and arranging permission from the S&C line manager based at Settle station, whose name I sadly cannot recall. The manager was extremely supportive of our desire to place the seat in the gravel area with the only stipulation that it had to be fixed and could not be moved. We record our grateful thanks to him.

Support crew member Graeme Page spoke to his dad Jimmy Page (not of Led Zeppelin fame) and he donated his garden seat, which was a former station seat, and we bought him a new replacement. I took it apart and had the metal legs sandblasted and protectively painted courtesy of Rippin's at the former Auchtermuchty railway station. Lindsay's eldest son, Alistair, supplied hardwood to make the seat and back. I set to work building the seat.

With the seat all finished we arranged an unveiling at Appleby for 16 April 1994 as A4 4498 would be present taking water on a southbound tour. A week before, Johnnie and I took the seat down to build it and to pour two cement anchors in the ground to attach it to. We left the seat covered over inside the brick water tower base for the week.

On a warm and very sunny 16 April we set off in convoy with several cars and a hired minibus as we had Jean, Lindsay's widow, and Alistair and his wife with

No. 4498 *Sir Nigel Gresley* stands in sunny Appleby station before the unveiling of Lindsay's seat. We couldn't have wished for a better day. (Michael Mather)

Lindsay's widow, Jean, and son Alistair unveil Lindsay's seat. (Michael Mather)

In memory of Lindsay Spittal, chief engineer of A4 Pacific 60009 *Union of South Africa*. From Support Crew and Friends. (Jules Hathaway)

An almost unique photograph, which includes all of the 1990s support crew. We were very rarely all together in one photograph. From back left: Jules, Mike, Fraser, Davy, Marilyn, John, DJ, Colin and Ian. Front: Graeme, Alistair's wife Alison, Jean, Alistair and Nick. (Michael Mather)

us for the unveiling. On arrival everyone, bar Johnnie and myself, went to the pub while we set about fixing the seat to the anchor bolts and covering it over. 4498 ran in, performed run pasts and was watered etc., and while it sat there we all gathered round and Colin said a few words in Lindsay's memory, then Jean uncovered the seat with its brightly polished brass plaque. Afterwards we retired to a nearby hotel for an afternoon tea before most of us headed home. Davy and a few others stayed the night in the hotel.

The seat was well looked after by the station staff and volunteers at Appleby and the wood was replaced at one point too. But the weather and time took its toll on the seat and it was removed, but not before the plaque was removed for our safe keeping. On every southbound trip we did afterwards we would sit and raise a cup of tea to our dear Lindsay while 'resting our weary arses'.

To absent friends.

Jules Hathaway

Over the years Number 9 and The Great Marquess stopped at Appleby for water and the support crew could make use of the seat. Here, Number 9 arrives at Appleby with a southbound Cumbrian Mountain Express in August 2004. (Michael Mather)

The Elizabethan

The story of the Elizabethan that Number 9 hauled in October 1994 goes back to the previous winter, when we were carrying out a piston and valve exam at Markinch. John had just removed the front cover from the centre cylinder when he discovered a crack in the cylinder liner.

This would mean the replacement of the liner, a job that couldn't be done at Markinch. Arrangements were made for Number 9 to travel to the Severn Valley Railway for repairs.

This took a number of weeks to arrange and it wasn't until May that Number 9 made the long journey to Bridgnorth on a low-loader. Little did we know it at the time but, as Number 9 trundled down Markinch high street, it would never return to the goods shed. The Severn Valley Railway became its base for the next thirteen years.

The journey by road meant crossing the Forth Road bridge, something Number 9 had done the year before when travelling to the Llangollen Railway, making it the only steam locomotive to have crossed both Forth bridges. It remains to be seen whether Nine ever crosses the new Queensferry Crossing!

While Number 9 was under repair at Bridgnorth, and with the onset of rail privatisation and open access to routes, *Steam Railway* magazine hatched a plan for a steam-hauled train departing from London Kings Cross and travelling up the east coast main line to Peterborough.

This would be the first steam-hauled train to leave Kings Cross since the Flying Scotsman in 1969 and was to be titled the Elizabethan. There was to be no difficulty in the choice of locomotive – it had to be Number 9, a locomotive that had hauled this non-stop London to Edinburgh service with distinction and indeed had hauled the first and last southbound train in 1953 and 1961 respectively, sharing the last day with 60022 *Mallard*, which hauled the final northbound run.

The date of the trip was to be 29 October, thirty years and five days since Number 9 had hauled what was supposed to be the last steam working from Kings Cross, The Jubilee Requiem, to Newcastle and return. So great was the demand for tickets on the Elizabethan that a second train was to run on 30 October.

By early October the repairs were complete and Number 9 emerged from the Bridgnorth workshops with the 1950s British Railways Cycling Lion badge on the

Standing beside the former Haig's whisky building and safely chained onto Allelys low-loader, Nine is ready to start the long trip to Bridgnorth on 17 May 1994. (Jules Hathaway)

Heading the up Elizabethan in August 1961, Number 9 passes through Grantham station. (Colour-Rail)

tender and a black background to the nameplates. It has always been a matter of fierce debate among the support crew as to what is the best colour for the nameplates, red or black. Even Scottish Region blue has been suggested!

To get Number 9 to London, a tour, the Capital Streak, had been organised, which Nine would haul from Worcester to London Paddington before moving to Bounds Green depot to be prepared for the Elizabethan. This trip also gave the London drivers a chance to get the feel of the loco before the big day, getting on at Reading for the last part of the trip.

With some of the support crew already in London, the rest of us, Davy, Colin and myself, made our way down on the Friday night and an early start was made on the Saturday morning to prepare Number 9 for its big day. Nine moved from Old Oak Common on the Thursday and in the process, according to Rail Track, caused a near flashover, whatever that is, while passing through Primrose Hill tunnel – something that would cause serious problems for us the following week.

And so the big day arrived and Nine had moved off shed with driver Ron Kennedy and fireman Dave Rollins in charge. Ron, in particular, was a true gentleman, making himself known to the support crew and also presenting us all with a badge each, which portrayed the coat of arms of his local council, which he was proud to be a councillor on. Ron had another claim to fame, having been the fireman on the V2 that played a starring role along with Herbert Lom in the Ealing comedy *The Ladykillers*.

Number 9 was soon coupled up to the train, which consisted of twelve coaches including the support coach behind the loco and an officers' saloon at the rear.

Severn Valley general manager Alun Rees, John Cameron, fireman Dave Rollins and driver Ron Kennedy pose with Number 9 at Bounds Green depot. (David Murray)

Crowds gather at Kings Cross to witness an historic occasion – the first A4 to depart for thirty years, and the first steam departure since 1969. (Michael Mather)

The whole lot was dragged down to Kings Cross by a Class 47 diesel and we were greeted by a huge crowd on Platform 1, including distinguished guests – former Kings Cross and Stewarts Lane shedmasters Peter Townend and Dick Hardy respectively, along with a number of retired former Kings Cross enginemen who would travel in the officers' saloon. We were soon ready for our 09.30 departure.

Leaving 'The Cross', Ron took it steady on the climb through Gas Works and Copenhagen tunnels and up Holloway bank. Sadly, we weren't taking the east coast main line proper but going via the Hertford loop, rejoining the ECML at Langley junction.

It was now meet the passengers time, as we had commemorative mugs for sale, black for the Saturday and blue for the Sunday, which would keep two of us busy on the trip to Peterborough. It is always good to meet the passengers and even better to get them to part with some of their money, but the highlight for me was meeting Alan Pegler, saviour of *Flying Scotsman*. I didn't have the nerve to charge him for a mug, bearing in mind all he had done for main line running and preservation.

On arrival at Peterborough Number 9 ran round it's train and then dragged it tender first onto the Nene Valley Railway to Wansford, where it would be turned and serviced before working a service train on the line before returning to Peterborough station with its train ready for the return journey, this time with driver Ron Edmunds and fireman Tony Applegarth on the footplate. Ron was soon to retire and said it was the best farewell present he could have had.

On this trip we didn't have our own support coach with its well-equipped kitchen, just a double-burner stove and too few pots to cook our evening meal. The peas were cooked in the frying pan, after which Marilyn decided to get rid of the pea water out of the window – she didn't shout 'gardiloo' to warn Davy, who was a few windows down and ended up getting an eyeful. Or rather his glasses did!

And so a good run back to London through the darkness was enjoyed by all, but the excitement for the support crew wasn't over yet.

By the time we arrived at Kings Cross the tender was very low on water, there not being enough for the rather protracted return to Bounds Green. So, despite protestations from the station manager, who wanted us out of his station, we set about finding a hydrant, of which there were plenty – but we couldn't fit our standpipe to any as the water outlets were out of line with the manholes. Goodness knows what they would have done if there was a fire. So there we were running up and down the platform like blue ***** flies looking for a hydrant, eventually finding one we could use outside the station. We still laugh about that.

There now started the lengthy trip to Bounds Green, which took ages, and we were all sitting in the support coach shattered by the long day and with it all to do again tomorrow, when we got a rude awakening as we passed through the carriage wash!

Luckily for the Sunday run Number 9 only needed normal preparation for the trip, no problems having occurred.

Once again Ron Kennedy was in charge for the run to Peterborough and this time, having got the hang of the engine, made a more spirited climb of Holloway Bank.

On arrival at Wansford John and I bid our farewells as we now had to return home in order to be back at work on the Monday morning and so left the remaining support crew to do the return trip, which they reported was as good as Saturday's, and no water problems at Kings Cross.

We did a roaring trade selling these mugs that were supplied by Davy's cousin David Murray. The black one was for the Saturday and the blue for Sunday. (Michael Mather Collection)

Colin being interviewed by the local television station while we were at Wansford on the Nene Valley Railway. (Michael Mather)

The Elizabethan weekend has got to be one of the best times I have had with Number 9 and the support crew have only one regret about the weekend – that Lindsay wasn't with us. He had always had an ambition to take Nine to London, but sadly didn't live to see it happen.

Postscript:
On arrival back at Bounds Green on the Sunday night Number 9 was impounded by Rail Track following the alleged 'near flashover' at Primrose Hill, pending investigations, and remained there for three weeks before being released and moving to Crewe Heritage Centre ready to work a Cumbrian Mountain Express to Carlisle in December.

Michael Mather

Bank, what Bank?

We had a great run the day before from Clapham Junction to Exeter down the LSWR route and today we were going back to London via the GWR. Alun Rees was telling us we had a stiff climb ahead up Whiteball Bank to the summit at the tunnel with Wellington bank on the other side.

We were looking forward to a good run. The inspector was Ian Davies, fireman was Des Walker and the driver was former Marylebone legend Trevor Barnett. This was Trevor's last steam trip.

We departed Exeter St David's station and Trevor soon got the loco into its stride without a trace of a slip with eleven bogies weighing in at some 435 tons on the drawbar. It was soon very clear that Trevor was going to have 'a very good last trip' as he was not hanging about.

At Hele we were running beside the M5 and going faster than the cars on the motorway, so the speed was in the high 70s. I looked back down the train and the exhaust was hanging in the air and I thought, 'Where's this bank Reesy was on about?' Then Graeme came off the footplate and said I should go up, so I did.

Ian Davies was firing, and I asked him 'Where are we?' He replied but I couldn't hear; he looked out and said something else inaudible. We were doing over 70 mph. We went over the summit and into Whiteball Tunnel and started down Wellington Bank. Still Trevor kept the steam on and the sparks from the lum streaked past. We came out like a bullet from a gun and the speed was into the 80s now. John Cameron went over and said to Trevor to lengthen the cut-off slightly as the loco was choking; he did and we went faster still. The speedo crept up to 90 and passed it, then passed 95 and as it neared the ton Ian put his hand on Trevor's shoulder and that was it all over. Arrival at the Taunton water stop was 4 and a half minutes early and virtually the whole train surrounded the loco to applaud Mr Barnett for the best 75 mph they had ever experienced.

The ton! (Fraser Birrell Collection)

TABLE 12
THE DEVONIAN STREAK
EXETER ST DAVID'S TO BRISTOL T.M.

Date	:-	19.2.95
Loco	:-	60009 'Union of South Africa'
Load	:-	11
Tons tare/gross	:-	413 / 435
Driver	:	Trevor Barnett
Fireman	:-	Des Walker
Depot	:-	Exeter
Inspector	:-	Ian Davies
Weather	:-	Calm, rail damp, heavily overcast, light rain from Tiverton Parkway on.

Dist m.c.	Timing Point	Booked m.secs	Actual m.secs	Speed m.p.h.
0.00	**EXETER ST DAVIDS**	**0.00**	**0.00**	-
1.19	Cowley Bridge Jucn.	3.00	4.01	42
3.32	Stoke Canon		6.30	61
5.32	Milepost 188½		8.21	70/72
6.72	Milepost 187		9.37	71
8.31	Hele LC		10.51	73
10.72	Milepost 183		12.54	75
12.45	Cullompton		14.12	78
14.32	Milepost 179½		15.38	74
14.65	Tiverton Junction		15.57	81/82
16.46	Tiverton Parkway	19.00	17.16	80
17.72	Milepost 176		18.16	78
18.32	Milepost 175½		18.40	74
18.72	Milepost 175		19.04	74
19.12	Burlescombe		19.16	74
19.52	Milepost 174¼		19.41	71
19.72	Milepost 174		19.54	70
20.59	Whiteball Tunnel (Out)		20.34	84/95
23.52	Wellington		22.31	85
26.20	Bradford Crossing		24.28	76
28.61	Norton Fitzwarren		26.30	63
			t.s.r.	
29.37	Silk Mill Junction		27.21	38
30.61	**TAUNTON**	**35.00**	**30.08**	-
0.00	**TAUNTON**	**0.00**	**0.00**	-
2.31	Creech Junction		5.11	57
4.56	Cogload Junction	6.00	7.19	70
5.54	Durston		8.07	73½
7.11	Milepost 156		9.14	81/82
10.51	Milepost 152½		11.50	80
11.43	Bridgwater	13.00	12.29	83/84
14.11	Milepost 149		14.22	82/84
16.11	Huntspill		15.50	81/83
17.66	Highbridge		17.04	82/81
20.51	Brent Knoll		19.08	82
22.71	Milepost 140¼		20.44	85
			signals	
24.43	Bleadon & Uphill		23.03	22
25.06	Uphill Junction	33.00	24.06	37/48
			signal stop	
	Signal B11 (MP 135½)		29.02	-
			35.56	-
28.00	Worle Junction	34.00	38.02	28
29.12	Puxton & Worle LC		39.49	46
30.79	Huish LC		41.54	59
32.65	Yatton		43.40	64
34.11	Milepost 129		44.52	67/70½
36.58	Nailsea & Blackwell		47.05	69½/70
38.71	Flax Bourton		48.58	67½
40.11	Milepost 123		50.05	67½
41.17	Long Ashton		50.55	69
42.11	West Depot		51.50	66½
42.70	Parson Street		52.40	56
43.71	Bedminster		54.15	23
44.31	Bristol West Junction		55.48	16
44.61	**BRISTOL T.M. (Plat. 4)**	**56.00**	**58.39**	-

Well-respected train timer, the late Mike Notley's speed table for the record run. (Ian Leven Collection)

The run on to Bristol saw speeds in the mid-80s and our driver could hang up his main line grease top having gone out in style with the fastest preserved steam run. But things were to change.

After a prolonged water stop at Bristol Temple Meads station, we departed just over an hour late. A pilotman boarded due to wrong line working past a derailed wagon in an engineering possession. On the 2-mile 1 in 75 climb past Ashley Hill we slipped to a stand. Several restarts failed and hand-sanding took place with Alun Rees driving to get the train moving. At one point the loco blew off and the poor pilotman (who'd never been on a steam loco before) produced a lovely litter of kittens! He was dropped off at Filton Junction and we got going passing Hullavington at 86 mph.

Davy Murray's wish of a two-fingered whistle blow at speed on the fast through line at Swindon was thwarted by a hot box detector and we were stopped on the fast for examination. Nothing found. Restarting we were 2 and quarter hours late and it was decided we would come off at Didcot.

Little did the support crew know when preparing Number 9 that history was about to be made during Nine's flight down from Whiteball. (Jules Hathaway)

With the loco put to bed at GWS Didcot, the support crew repaired to the Station Hotel for a well-earned celebratory pint or two and a reflection of the historic day that had just occurred, with the fastest speed recorded behind a steam loco since 1967 by an LNER loco on a GWR route… Gresley Was Right!

Jules Hathaway

At the NRM

The National Railway Museum in York is a Mecca for all rail enthusiasts and a renowned repository for all railway items, not just locos and rolling stock. It also boasts a host of engineering and servicing facilities.

For the main line steam loco these facilities are made available to allow locomotives to be based at York for rail tours starting or finishing at the station. Until recently there was 24-hour security staff with entry and exit to the sidings outside via the tradesmen entrance and by walking through the Great Hall to the door by the sidings. This gave a unique access to the main part of the museum when closed to the public. Returning to the coach in the evening meant walking through the Great Hall with most of the lights switched off. This brought an experience not felt during the day. The atmosphere was knee deep and it swirled around the exhibits like mist and to spend time in there was breathtaking. The security staff were wonderful and allowed us to take photos and linger for as long as we liked.

Above left: All my own work, a fine plume of smoke rises from Nine's lum as it stands on the NRM turntable. (Michael Mather)

Above right: From left: Dave Judd, Davy and John enjoy a light-hearted moment in the cab of *Green Arrow* at the NRM on 5 October 1996. Dave Judd, or DJ as we called him as we had two Davids, joined us in 1991. A college lecturer with great patience, he put us through our first aid course! A keen outdoor enthusiast, he sadly passed away while out hill walking on Boxing Day 2006. (Michael Mather)

Two occasions for me always raises a smile and a laugh.

On 5 October 1996 we worked a tour from Peterborough to York and return. On arrival at York we were booked to go into the museum to turn on the operational turntable – quite a spectacle. We were waiting to go into the Great Hall, I was on the footplate and the fire was just about out, so I put six good shovels of coal right along the back to keep it burning. Just before moving off Richard Gibbon, the head of engineering, comes on the footplate jumping up and down about the amount of smoke we were making. I told him the fire was about out and I didn't want to lose steam and sit down on the turntable. The driver made a comment in support of me and Mr Gibbon stormed off. The driver took us in, we turned and went out leaving a very atmospheric aroma in the building for some time afterwards.

Coming forward to 20 August 2007 and this time I do it in style! The loco is on the single prep road with walls on three sides and two large extractor fans in the roof. The fire is lit, I'm trying to raise steam and there is more smoke coming out of the cab than the chimney. After many hours not much is happening, and I enquire about getting towed out to get air about the loco. There's no driver I'm told. A bit later one of the officials comes out to ask if the extractor fans are on as they have closed part of the museum due to smoke. I said yes and asked again about being towed out. A short time later he is back saying the smoke had set off the fire alarms, the museum had been evacuated and the fire service were in attendance. Oops. My response was I had asked twice about being towed out. Ten minutes later a shunter appears and drags the loco out. 30 minutes after that I had steam!

Later in the evening when walking through to go out for a meal there was a faint hint of smoke in the very top of the roof and a wonderful atmospheric aroma. Talking to the wonderful security guys later on, they just laughed it off.

Jules Hathaway

Air Brakes and Going Continental

Above: Number 9's second overhaul at the Severn Valley Railway was completed in 2001 and it was at this time that an air brake system was fitted. The air pump seen here, which came from Poland, was mounted between the rear driving axle and the firebox, the only practical place it could go. (Davy Murray)

Right: When first introduced, the five empire A4s carried the coat of arms of the country they were named after on the cab side below the number. This feature was reinstated to Number 9 in 2001. The coat of arms was hand-painted at the Severn Valley. (Davy Murray)

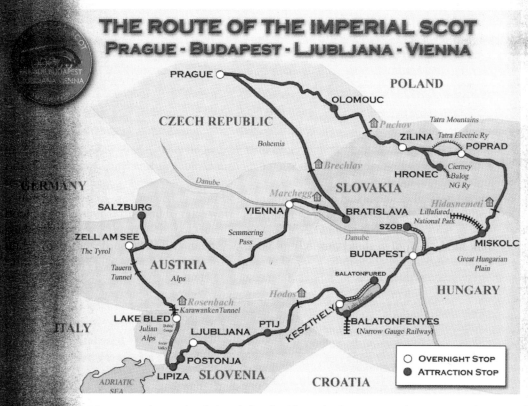

Because Number 9 was newly overhauled and fitted with air brakes, it was chosen to work a most ambitious European tour, the Imperial Scot, which was to run for two weeks in September 2001 and start and finish in Prague. Of course, Nine had first to get to Prague, a week's journey, by ferry to Rotterdam, then engine and coach across Europe. It was to be quite an adventure that we were all up for, but unfortunately didn't happen – first it was postponed to 2002, then it was cancelled. (Michael Mather Collection)

Number 9 heads south on the West Coast main line through the beautiful Lune Gorge on 2 August 2003. (Davy Murray)

Davy Murray

I first met Davy Murray when he was introduced to Thornton Model Railway Club by Willie Young, a running foreman at Thornton MPD. A shy teenager, he soon fitted in with us.

On the loco's return to main line working he became the right-hand man to Lindsay Spittal, our chief engineer. When Lindsay died in 1993 Davy became his natural successor. During our years at both Thornton and Markinch he led from the front, whether working on the loco or adding his name first to the crew list for any trips. A plumber by trade, he nevertheless grew to know every nut, bolt and pipe that made up the inner workings of the engine. When she moved to Bridgnorth in 1994 he organised the weekend gangs who, once or twice a month, went to prep the engine for trips. Such was his dedication, he often made solo trips south to help with minor repairs. Little wonder that he would disconnect the speedometer on his car to save clocking up excess mileage!

We were a close-knit gang, often playing tricks on each other, and it would be remiss of me not to relate the tale when, at Carlisle Upperby, we were relaxing in the kitchen of the support coach after a trip, enjoying a dram or two. No one had noticed Davy disappearing when a ghostly voice was heard through the corridor tender – 'This is the voice of Sir Nigel Gresley, you will paint your engine BLUE!' Davy at his best!

In January 2007 Davy was diagnosed with an inoperable brain tumour and lost the battle for his life in August that year. Having become well-known in heritage railway circles, he was given a whole-page glowing tribute by David Wilcock in *Steam Railway* magazine.

From a shy youth to a giant of a man! RIP Davy.

Colin Cant

The late Davy Murray in a typical pose, with oil cans at the ready. (David Wilcock)

The Great Gathering

The great gathering of the six surviving A4s in July 2013, to celebrate the seventy-fifth anniversary of *Mallard*'s record-breaking run, was a fantastic event that drew huge crowds. Luckily, we were able to take our photographs after the museum closed for the night. Here, in the original Garter Blue livery, are Nos 4464 *Bittern*, 4468 *Mallard* and 4489 *Dominion of Canada*. (Michael Mather)

Representing the BR liveries, Dark Blue and Brunswick Green, and standing in numerical order are Nos 60007 *Sir Nigel Gresley*, 60008 *Dwight D. Eisenhower*, and 60009 *Union of South Africa*. (Michael Mather)

Is That a Woman on the Footplate?

This is a story of one woman's journey through main line steam preservation, in the company of a huge steam locomotive (60009 *Union of South Africa*) and the humans who have made its history over the last thirty years I have experienced as a support crew member.

Looking back, I was a very unlikely member of a support crew in 1989. In fact, it was never my intention to do any more than help with the renovation of the Mark 1 Brake that John Cameron had bought to be done up while Number 9 was being overhauled. I was invited by friends who were already part of the support crew to turn up at the railway shed in Markinch one Saturday with my upholstery shampooer. Over the next year I cleaned, scraped, washed and painted the coach and formed a lifelong bond with the wonderful group of men who gave their time to make sure Number 9 was always available for the jobs its owner wanted.

The chief engineer in 1990 when Number 9 came back onto the main line for the Forth Bridge centennial was Lindsay Spittal and he was always supportive of me even though having a woman on the footplate was unusual then. In fact, he told me there was a rule 'No skirts on the footplate'. I asked if that applied to kilts as well, as we were all Scottish except for one Englishman who is an honorary Scotsman and does wear a kilt. I knew by the amused glint in his eye that I had said the right thing and I was 'in'. I always called Lindsay 'dad' even though he wasn't really old enough and he called me daughter to the confusion of many a rail buff on platforms and trains.

I had no experience of main line steam and no engineering background, but I was willing to learn. And learn I did. I had to quickly learn tolerance for bad language and flatulence, as well as all the railway knowledge. I never asked for any concessions and none were given. I had to shovel coal same as the men. My lack of experience meant I did not know the alarming number of terms and tool names that were everyday terminology. What on earth was a dander shovel or a 9/16ths flogging spanner?

Because all the repairs and maintenance for the engine were done by the support crew in our own shed, I was not restricted to cleaning when I started. I cleaned out the

The newly painted support coach stands in Markinch shed in February 1990. The paintwork was done by railway photographer, professional painter and good friend of ours, the late Ian Smith. (Marilyn Leven)

I am never happier than when I am talking to enthusiasts and the public about our locomotive, but the guy in the bunnet seems to be doing all the talking here. (Marilyn Leven Collection)

smokebox and the firebox a lot. Especially as being smaller than the men I fitted easily into small spaces like behind the screens in the smokebox or through the firebox door.

Once I was in the firebox when it was still hot not long after the fire had been cleaned and dropped through the drop grate. I was shovelling ash from the back corners of the box when the cinders suddenly burst into flames. I got out a lot faster than I had come in by diving arms first through the door and banging my head on the cab floor.

The constant maintenance and repairs meant I found myself assisting to change tender springs and brake blocks, clean valve rings or strip down the motion. Any job that needed to be done, the support crew would do it. It was a great place to learn. I also had to learn the craft of taking an engine on the main line. Rolling out and taking in fire hoses, laying out electrical cables once a power supply was found for the engine and coach, trimming coal or oiling up became second nature.

I quickly realised that putting up with very early rises, being hot and dirty or cold and dirty and working long shifts came with the job – but I never, ever, thought of giving up.

The first time I did a main line trip as a full support crew member in my new blue bib and brace and jacket and still shiny steel toecap boots was the proudest of my life. The other members of the support crew inducted me by dirtying my boots. I was told 'Never clean your boots,' and I never have.

The most wonderful thing for me was being taught to fire. I had very able tutors and was given a copy of the black *Engineman's Handbook*. This book tells you everything you need to know about steam locomotives but not how to do anything. So, I learned on the job. I still get a thrill from laying and lighting the fire even now and the singing noise steam locos make as the water begins to boil is better than birdsong.

The chance to do a firing turn from Cumbernauld to our shed in Thornton was one I will always treasure. Especially as it meant firing over the Forth Bridge. These opportunities were scarce though as I had a full-time job and not as much time with my full-time hobby I would have liked.

Number 9 was used for crew training of ScotRail engine crew in the 1993. This was done on weekdays as well as weekends and I could not get time off. I volunteered to be at the shed in Markinch at 07.30 every morning to lock up once the engine was away before I went into work. All went well until one morning when the support crew, who were sleeping in the coach, slept in. I knocked loudly on all the compartment doors to wake them then found myself in skirt and high heels putting a poker through the fire and putting coal on while they got dressed. Luckily the engine was good at keeping its heat overnight and there was enough steam to move by the time the crew arrived at 08.00.

Staying overnight in railway depots was always a great source of fun as the exclusively male preserves were not suitable for women then and had no facilities. I got used to stares and comments, but I was never prevented from doing anything, although there seemed to be an assumption that any woman with the engine was there to make the tea and not to strip down steam sanders or oil up.

Number 9 takes the Glasgow line at Hilton Junction on 18 October 1993, with one of the crew training runs, which ran from Perth to Glasgow and return, that were open to the public. Two members of the support crew passed out as drivers at this time: Fraser Birrell and George Beattie. (Scott McGachy)

My male support crew always put anyone right, as well as providing a guard in the shower room.

In 1995 I married my husband, who of course was in the support crew. All the lads came to the wedding and provided a guard of honour, with suitably cleaned firing shovels, for the bride and groom.

Inevitably the engine had to have another full overhaul in 1998. This was a strain on all of us as the engine was 350 miles away at the Severn Valley Railway. Our home became the group's meeting place. We all got together every Monday night without fail to keep each other updated and organise who could manage to travel south. I am sure that the group may have drifted apart without this support. Once the engine was ready for the main line again there was a full support crew ready to go.

Then, just when we thought we had enough to do, Mr Cameron bought another engine in 2003. *The Great Marquess*, No. 61994 – a K4. I immediately fell in love with it. A K4 is an A4 in miniature and it appeared as if it was made just for me. The lack of streamlining made oiling up easier and all the controls in the cab could be reached without standing on a box in front of the fire. Unlike Number 9 there was no air pump either. I know this restricted the work that could be done but I was transported back to the good old days when I first started. Air pumps are necessary now for the air-braked carriages on the main line. This was not the case in my early career, and I have a heartfelt dislike of the thumping beat.

Suited and booted, the support crew provide a guard of honour with suitably polished firing shovels at our wedding on 13 May 1995. A surprise wedding gift from the crew was an engraved chrome-plated firing shovel! (Ian and Marilyn Leven Collection)

A great thing was the *Marquess* was built for the challenging gradients in the west highlands, so it could do the Fort William to Mallaig runs. Meeting all the foreign tourists and the spectacular scenery made up for the long days and hard work. A Spanish family were absolutely delighted to have a photograph of me and my support crew buddies eating fish and chips. Who would have known we would be a national icon? A young Japanese couple weren't interested in the engine at all. They wanted to see inside the '*Harry Potter*' coach attached. I explained this was our mobile home and not a film prop.

Having two main line engines meant that the support crew were severely stretched at times. Getting the K4 ready when there were as few as two was perhaps bad enough, but trying to get an A4 ready with only two is an exhausting business. No wonder the engine went out dirty sometimes.

Speaking about dirty, I was sharing a seat in the sunshine on the platform at Preston with Mr Cameron last year. *Union of South Africa*'s casing in front of us was not clean, except for the nameplates and Springbok that I had managed to polish in the early hours after I had finished filling the siphon boxes. Midweek running had proved a problem in getting sufficient support crew. He looked at the loco and turned with a smile on his face. 'That is how I remember them' he said. He didn't mind a jot that the engine was grubby.

All support crews must have a responsible officer on the day of a main line run that ensures the engine is fit to run and all the paperwork is done and signed by the driver. They must also make sure the members of the support crew have a valid PTS and are fit for duty. I never thought this person would be me and the first time I was given this responsibility a couple of years ago my stomach was churning and my knees were weak. I must have been ok though because I have done this job many times since.

Now my railway career is coming to a close my best memory has to be the day on 9 September 2015 when the Queen opened the new Borders Railway from Edinburgh to Tweedbank. Number 9 was the engine chosen to draw the royal train and was stabled overnight at Millerhill depot before moving to Waverley in the morning. I was the support crew fireman that morning so I can legitimately say I raised steam on the royal train.

Most of Number 9's work in the last five years has been south of the border and I am glad that now being retired means I can travel south as often as I want. The engine is always greeted with enthusiasm on our trips out of London and the public seem delighted that a Scottish woman is on the support crew.

My fantastic hobby has taken me from Inverness to Devon and from Scarborough to Anglesey.

Doing main line trips, open days, visits to preserved lines and depots and thousands of hours spent in the support coach with a marvellous group of like-minded people has produced enough material for several books, I am sure. I want to thank the men and, now, other women in the support crew and the greater preservation world for allowing me to be part of it all. A special thanks of course to John Cameron for not only providing the railway world with two marvellous steam engines but for never doubting my ability to be part of the support crew.

Marilyn Leven

The Jubilee Requiem

On 24 October 1964 Number 9 hauled the Jubilee Requiem rail tour from London Kings Cross to Newcastle and return. This was supposed to be the last ever steam-hauled train from Kings Cross. It is seen here at Newcastle Central station. (Robin Barbour, courtesy of Bruce McCartney)

On 25 October 2014 history repeated itself when Number 9 again left Kings Cross at the head of the Jubilee Requiem for Newcastle, but only worked back as far as York. With a 75 mph speed limit and having to run between other services, a return to Kings Cross wasn't practical, so an electric locomotive took over at York. Nine is seen here again at Newcastle Central station. (Michael Mather)

The Royal Train

Ask any main line loco owner what would be the pinnacle of their time with the loco and many, if not all, would say that the opportunity to haul a train for the Queen would be their ultimate dream. I know that John Cameron always hoped that this would be possible for Number 9 and it was a regular topic with the support crew. We had seen the opportunity arise for other preserved locos and always hoped it would happen to us.

When the new line from Edinburgh to Tweedbank was built we heard the rumour that the Queen would be opening it and suddenly realised that we were the most obvious choice to be involved. When we heard from Mr Cameron that we had indeed been granted the honour, it felt that all our dreams had come true.

It may seem that this would be a simple operation but that is not the case. Many weeks of preparation were required to ensure that each support crew member who would be on duty that day had their background checked and no one had any terrorist leanings! The loco was in Crewe just prior to the trip and had to be moved to Edinburgh along with the Pullman carriage, which would be used by the Queen on the day. The loco and the stock were assembled at Millerhill and thoroughly searched, using police sniffer dogs, to ensure that no suspect packages had been secreted aboard.

On the day of the opening, 9 September 2015, the support crew were up very early to ensure everything was in order and the train was hauled up to Edinburgh Waverley.

60009 *Union of South Africa* climbs past Tyne Head on the long climb to Falahill summit with the Borders Railway opening Royal Train. Her Majesty the Queen, the Duke of Edinburgh and Scotland's First Minister Nicola Sturgeon travelled in the Pullman coach 'Pegasus' coupled behind the support coach. The Class 67 diesel on the rear of the train was required to haul the train back to Edinburgh as there are no turning facilities at Tweedbank. (Michael Mather)

Throughout September and October 2015 Number 9 hauled a series of trips to Tweedbank, and here John Graham of the A4 Locomotive Society is seen building up the fire at Millerhill depot where Nine was stabled at this time. John has been a great help to us over the years with his technical knowledge. (Jules Hathaway)

Looking over John Cameron's shoulder to the line ahead as Number 9 climbs up to Falahill summit on 27 September 2015. (Michael Mather)

All smiles at Tweedbank from Mike, Colin, Wilma Wilson (John Cameron's PA) and John. This was the last of the Borders Railway trips, 18 October 2015. (Robert Wilson)

Although it was a beautiful sunny day in Edinburgh there had been a heavy fog at Balmoral, where the Queen was residing. This meant that her helicopter flight to Holyrood, her Edinburgh residence, was delayed and she suffered a further setback when the roads had been closed for a bike race. She arrived at Waverley some 90 minutes late, but this did not dismay the assembled crowds who waved and cheered on her arrival.

Everything else on the day went according to plan and memories of the trip become hazy as we became caught up in the euphoria of the occasion. On arrival at Tweedbank there were the usual ceremonies to open the station and it seemed no time at all before the royal party were whisked off for lunch. They would not be returning by train but the invited guests had to be conveyed back to Edinburgh. The occasion may only have lasted a few hours but will remain in my memory forever.

The support crew is very proud to be involved with Number 9 and the royal train.

Colin Cant

Hospitality

Number 9's support crew has been rightly credited with being generous and friendly to anyone interested in the loco from the time it was bought by Mr Cameron. Having a support coach from 1990 meant there was more opportunity for interaction with the travelling public or guests who were invited along. Mr Cameron always had friends or business acquaintances that he wanted to show off his pride and joy to. This meant the support crew becoming catering staff for the VIPs, but tea and rolls were always given with a smile.

Being chairman of ScotRail in the early days, Mr Cameron was able to provide the support crew with travel passes like the railway company staff had. This meant everyone could travel free to where the engine was stabled at the time. Travelling together as a group was a laugh-a-minute joy. Once a trip to Carlisle saw us all in the vestibule of a train because it was so busy there were no seats left. We were all sitting on the floor outside the toilet. Our youngest member had to use the facilities and locked the door of the cubicle. Knowing he was petrified of spiders someone drew a spider on a slip of paper and pushed it under the door. Only silence came from inside then, to our disappointment, the piece of paper slid out under the door again with a large foot drawn on it stamping on the spider.

While Number 9 was on the move letting a select few onto the footplate was possible due to the corridor tender. The support crew were always rightly proud of this feature. The willing victims were kitted out usually in long railwayman's coats to keep their clothes clean. They were given a safety briefing by the RO then pointed up the corridor towards their host in his usual seat on the footplate. Most were thrilled at the experience, but one lady did beat a hasty retreat, her scream reverberating all the way out into the train. The intensity of the experience of the noise, heat and speed the engine was travelling at was just too much. Safety fears in recent times have made guests on the footplate a thing of the past. Anyone now on a footplate has to have a current Personal Track Safety certificate. The most we could do was allow the brave visitor along the corridor to look into the footplate. This was memorable for them though as the sounds, sights and smells were still experienced.

When the loco returned to the main line after overhaul in 1990 the support crew decided making a little money for things not covered by Mr Cameron's allowance would be a good idea. Having a sales trolley that could go through the train on the move selling excusive goods like maker's plates or badges was a great chance to not only make some funds but to meet the public. An old hostess trolley was procured, and everyone took turns at sales. Some support crew were more willing than others. On one occasion a nameless support crew member locked himself in the toilet rather than face it. He did give in eventually and, we think, enjoyed the experience once he got started.

A long-time fan of the engine, Peter Drummond had taken an excellent shot of the engine at speed. The group decided this would make an excellent postcard to sell and it was sent to the printers to be produced. The picture had been taken on the Settle to Carlisle line and was titled 'The Cumbrian Mountain Express'. Something got lost in translation though because the cards came back called 'The Caribbean Express'. Once we stopped laughing, we gave them away free.

Going through the train also gave the passengers a chance to talk to the support crew directly. We were often asked who was driving if we were not on the footplate. We always said the engine was on automatic pilot.

Some of the items we had for sale from our trolley. The postcard on the left by Jules shows Nine as *Osprey* in 1990 and on the right, by Peter Drummond, the one misprinted as *The Caribbean Express*! The miniature nameplates were made from melted-down worn-out brass bushes removed from the engine. (Michael Mather Collection)

Allowing the public on the footplate while we were stationary had always been enjoyable for the support crew and positively encouraged by Mr Cameron, who loved to pose for photographs. On the move the times at stations were limited but there have been many occasions when the loco has attended open days and events where whole days could be spent talking to enthusiasts, something I am never happier doing. The highlights have maybe been Doncaster, Crewe, the great gathering of the six A4s at the NRM and the great goodbye at Shildon.

The event at the NRM exceeded anyone's expectations at the numbers that came, and all the support crew gave days of their time to take turns talking to groups on the footplate and giving a history of the engine and how it works. People who were there commented on how great it was to listen to our talks and thanked us for the patience shown to children or very elderly relatives. There was a heatwave during the event, but even so the numbers attending exceeded 100,000, including old-timers who had driven the engines.

I was very encouraged by how many women attended, almost always with male companions or family. I started giving them the chance to sit in the driver's seat and learn the controls. The reactions were heart warming. None of the women ever thought they would get that opportunity.

Having the corridor tender also enabled the crew to be supplied with tea or even food on the move. Having a good meal every day had always been a ritual with the support crew from the early days. We would hear with horror how some support crews would be out all day with just sandwiches. No, we always had a hot meal, which would be

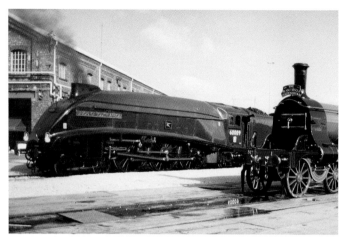

Doncaster Works open day on 26 July 2003 and two of its finest products, Number 9 and the Great Northern Railway Stirling Single No. 1, stand side by side. Visitors to the cab naturally wanted to blow the whistle and this was happening so often that Roland Kennington of *Flying Scotsman* came over and complained about the noise. Needless to say, the whistle kept blowing! (Davy Murray)

shared with any visitors in the coach as well. One visitor who was used to perhaps more fine dining was absolutely amazed that such a good meal could be produced from tins. Sitting down together to eat was good bonding and we discussed any problems or told funny stories of what had happened that day.

Our first chief engineer Lindsay Spittal was a great whisky connoisseur and many a time when we were off duty after a good day out he would produce a full bottle,

Crowds mob the National Railway Museum during the Great Gathering. (Michael Mather)

When John Cameron was chairman of ScotRail he would occasionally use his locomotive for official trips. In this view from 27 October 1991, Lindsay looks on as Number 9 stands in Edinburgh Waverley with an officers' saloon, ready to set off for Perth carrying, among others, the head of the French railways. (Michael Mather)

open it and throw the cork out of the window. No one would go to bed until it was drunk with many toasts and laughter. 'Here's tae us, wha's like us, gie few, an they're aw deed.' Towards the end of Number 9's career though, first thing in the morning it was more likely to be medication rather than hangover cures that were taken due to the support crew getting older and the rules on drinking being stricter.

The meal remembered with most affection while on the move has to be a Burns supper for ten. The cock-a-leekie soup was tinned, as was the haggis. The neeps and tatties had to be produced from scratch though, and two members had to hang onto the pots on the cooker as the engine gained speed over some rough track.

The support crew have held a Burns supper every January for the last thirty-one years, mostly at Marilyn and Ian's house. Kilts and poetry are still there, although a lot less whisky is drunk than in previous times. The cock-a-leekie soup is produced from scratch and is the traditional recipe with the addition of prunes. Not everyone likes prunes, so some swap them out of their bowls to those who do eat them. This passing of the prunes has now become a tradition. Colin does the 'address to the haggis' with the traditional large carving knife in his hand.

Like many other groups we also have a Christmas party. As hostess with a love of history and cooking, I always created a historic theme to the parties to make them a

Taking a break in the support coach kitchen while heading down the east coast main line are, at the back from left: Brian, George and Gordon. Front: Colin, Ian, Alexa Stott of the A1 Society and John Graham. (Phil Marsh)

bit different from the usual turkey and crackers. At the millennium in 2000 the party was set in the year 1000. The food was really unusual but tasty. Nothing from the New World of course, so no potatoes.

There has been a wartime Christmas with spam fritters and apple crumble, a Roman feast, a medieval feast and even dinner on the diner of a 1930s Chatanooga choo choo in the States. The party best remembered by all has to be first-class dining on the *Titanic*. This was a five course meal with wine and everyone in evening dress. The food was produced from the actual menu from the White Star liner. I was rescued by the RMS *Carpathia* late in the evening, but all the men went down with the ship. At least they looked like a shipwreck the next morning.

When the engine was away from its own shed doing a job in another part of the country it could be stabled in a railway yard or a suitable preserved railway shed overnight. Once all the prep work was done and the engine put to bed the support crew always headed out for a meal at a local restaurant. Mr Cameron always paid for this meal and there are many happy memories of favourite places. The logistics of getting a full support crew cleaned up to a standard that would allow them into a nice eatery when there was maybe just one shower cubicle for all of us is the stuff of legend.

It was not unknown for buckets of hot water from the boiler, via the injector overflow, to be used for ablutions in the coach toilet. Davy always said the water treatment in this hot water gave him a fine tanned look.

Through all the years the support crew in Scotland has always been a family sharing the good and bad times. There have been a great many changes over time, losses of old friends and gains of new support crew members. Of necessity new members have been from south of the border due to the amount of work the engine does there. From last year, the fact there was no longer an engine shed in Scotland was a loss keenly felt at the time but the crew kept on going.

Trying to look like 'The Fab Four' on the Abbey Road album cover, 'The Fab Five' – Colin, Mike, Brian, Marilyn and Ian – leave Thornton shed for the last time on 26 March 2018. The former diesel servicing shed had been the Scottish base of Number 9 and The Great Marquess since 2007, not that they were there very often. (Jules Hathaway)

A heartfelt thanks to all the supporters, public, private railway staff, railway company staff and family of the support crew who have made all the years with the engine enjoyable and memorable.

Tribute must also be paid to John Cameron's wife, Margaret, and his PA, Wilma Wilson, whose work and support behind the scenes have been invaluable to the running of the locomotive.

Marilyn Leven

The Great Britain

Number 9, and indeed *The Great Marquess* which John Cameron also owned by the time this round-Britain special train started running in 2007, have been regular performers over the years, mostly on the Scottish legs, but on occasion on legs out of or into 'Englandshire'.

The first edition in 2007 tied in with the two locomotives' return to Scotland after many years at the Severn Valley Railway and latterly Crewe, where *The Great Marquess* had recently been overhauled.

Taking over the train at Glasgow Central on 10 April, Number 9 hauled it to Perth where *The Great Marquess* was coupled on the front for the next section over the Highland main line to Inverness, where Nine had three days off – but the support crew and *The Marquess* didn't as they were off to Kyle of Lochalsh the next day. The pair hauled the return south to Perth on 14 April, where they came off and headed for their new home at Thornton.

The two locomotives were again rostered for Great Britain duty in 2013, Number 9 doing an Aberdeen to Edinburgh leg and *The Great Marquess* used from Thornton to Mallaig and return to Edinburgh, from where Nine took over for the first part of the return journey as far as York.

There being no operational turntable at Aberdeen, Nine had to be hauled up tender-first to the Granite City by a West Coast Class 37 that was a bit under the

On 14 April 2007 Number 9 and *The Great Marquess* power away from Dunkeld on the Highland main line, with the inaugural Great Britain tour. The *Marquess* was coupled inside as it developed a fault while heading to Kyle of Lochalsh the previous day. (Michael Mather)

Their job done for the day, John Cameron's two locomotives stand in the bay platform at Perth station while Jules holds The Great Britain headboard that had just been removed and was about to be fitted to the diesel that was taking over. (Michael Mather)

weather, Nine having to give it a wee hand occasionally. The run to Aberdeen was met by quite a few disappointed faces at the lineside as we passed, as the *Dundee Courier* had reported that Nine was going to Aberdeen for the first time in many years, but not that it would only be hauling the train south, the northbound run being hauled by a Black 5. On arrival at Aberdeen a tanker was waiting to top up the tender, soon after which the Black 5 arrived with The Great Britain.

Departing Aberdeen with West Coast driver Peter Walker at the regulator, Nine was soon into its stride, reportedly keeping to similar times to the famous 3-hour expresses of the 1960s, but with a heavier train.

This run south showed just how many people must read the *Dundee Courier* for there must have been hundreds of folk at the lineside to see us pass and the further south we went the more people there were, a huge crowd being at the south end of the Tay Bridge to witness Nine's last crossing of it. Needless to say, there was also a large crowd at Nine's old home at Markinch to see us charging past with the chime whistle sounding. It was so good to see so many people out to see us pass.

On arrival at Edinburgh Nine and support coach headed back to Thornton as the support coach was needed for the following three days by *The Great Marquess* for its part of The Great Britain to Fort William and Mallaig with half of the train, the other half heading to Kyle of Lochalsh behind a Black 5.

We weren't finished yet when *The Great Marquess* arrived back at Waverley, as Number 9 still had the Edinburgh to York leg to do the following day! I had to miss out on that as work beckoned.

The following year Number 9 was rostered for the Edinburgh to Inverness via Aberdeen and return, and Edinburgh to York sections of The Great Britain. Taking half the train to Inverness before going to Kyle the next day behind the K1, while the other half went to Mallaig, Nine had an easy trip to the Highland capital with such a light train, but the support crew were to have fun on arrival!

Stabled at Inverness adjacent to Network Rail's office cabins we made our normal request to plug our landline in and asked if we could use their toilet facilities, both of which were granted, but on the understanding that when the manager arrived in the morning they may not be so accommodating. He wasn't and unplugged our cable, threw it out and locked the door, which wasn't handy for me as I was in the toilet at the time! The lack of power we could get around, as we have a small generator, but the lack of a toilet was an inconvenience to say the least. In all our years of stabling at depots we have never been treated like this, and as a support crew we always leave any facilities as we would wish to find them.

Anyway, we had work to do, as on arrival at Inverness the firebox was full to the firehole door. The coal had not broken down to ash and cinders. There was only one way to get it out and that was the way it went in, a laborious and hot job that some support crew set about tackling. Gordon and I got lucky to start with anyway as we set about repairing a leaking gasket on the water feed to an injector, taking over from those on the footplate when we had finished, by which time it was possible for me to get into the firebox and shovel the cinders out. We all deserved our beers later that day!

The return to Edinburgh was punctuated by a scheduled long layover at Inverurie, during which time many of the locals came to see Number 9 – even the local press, who we dually posed for.

Above: Number 9 heads the Aberdeen to Edinburgh section of The Great Britain on 24 April 2013 at Forthar Bridge, on the climb from Ladybank to Lochmuir summit. (Scott McGachy)

Right: The ashes and clinker that were dug out of the firebox at Inverness on 2 May 2014. That was not fun. Gordon and John look on. (Michael Mather)

The following day saw Nine on its old stomping ground, heading south from Edinburgh. I was on the footplate when, as we charged through Dunbar at 75 mph, we received a message that the water tanker that was to meet us at Tweedmouth loop had broken down. This was serious, to say the least. Never daunted, a plan was hatched as we knew of a water hydrant in a street adjacent to Berwick north loop. Arrangements were made to go to Tweedmouth loop as planned, from where Nine and the support coach would go back to the north loop to take water from the hydrant that was six fire hoses away! Putting six hoses down is easy but emptying and rolling them up certainly isn't. Anyway, we got the water and rejoined the train.

With a water stop at Ferryhill from another tanker we arrived at York and handed over to *The Duchess* after an eventful few days.

The last occasion that Number 9 hauled The Great Britain was in 2019 when it was rostered for the Preston to Edinburgh and Edinburgh to Aberdeen and return legs.

Double-heading with Black 5 No. 44871 from Preston to Edinburgh the two locos made light work of Shap and Beattock.

It was touch and go as to whether Nine would get to Aberdeen as a serious steam leak in the firebox developed soon after arrival in Edinburgh. Monitored all night, it wasn't until the fire was built up in the morning that it sealed itself, to a sigh of relief from us all. This was an important trip as Nine was to be turned on the recently restored Aberdeen Ferryhill turntable. A television crew were also traveling with us, making an episode of *The Most Beautiful Railway* for Channel 4. They must have filmed everything that we did that day, most of it ending on the cutting room floor.

It was so good to do a return trip to Aberdeen again, even if we were a bit late on the return, but at least the late running meant we witnessed a beautiful sunset passing Stirling. A good way to finish Number 9's last run with this train.

Michael Mather

The Last Year

With just one year and one month to go, although we didn't know that then, Nine stands at Southall depot on 15 February 2019, being prepared for a tour to Worcester the following day. In the cab is Jamie Prince, one of our longest-serving members from south of the border. (Michael Mather)

Callum, Chris, Daryll, Fraser, Nicky and Marilyn stand beside Number 9 at York station on 15 February 2020, prior to departure for London on what would be Nine's last trip down the east coast main line. (Chris Boyd)

On what turned out to be its second last tour, deep in Great Western territory and about to start the climb of Sapperton bank, Number 9 storms past Brimscombe, Stroud, with a returning London Paddington to Worcester Cotswold Explorer tour, on 22 February 2020. (Shaz Lee)

The last arrival and the support crew pose for the cameras. Back from left: Mike, John, James, Jason, Marilyn, Nicky, Fraser, who was firing, and driver Peter Kirk. In front are the two Johns, Graham and Cameron. We had just arrived at York from Ealing Broadway via the Midland main line on what turned out to be Number 9's last main line tour on 7 March 2020. (Jason Brown)

This photograph should really have sound – 60009 *Union of South Africa* and support coach have just uncoupled from their last main line train and move away from York station with a very prolonged and poignant whistle, a moment that will remain in many a memory forever. It was hoped to run further tours in Scotland before the boiler certificate expired on 22 April, but Covid-19 put paid to that. (Don Brundell)

And so, having covered a total of 2,000,486 miles, the main line career of A4 Pacific 60009 *Union of South Africa* came to the end, after twenty-nine years with the LNER and BR and fifty-four years under John Cameron's ownership (including her six years at Lochty) during which time she covered a total of 156,758 miles, 1,000 of those at Lochty.

Fifty plus years we've lit the fire
It never was a chore
We never thought it would come to this
As we'll light the fire no more

Colin Cant

Acknowledgements

Although most of the photographs in this book are from the members of the support crew and from the collection of the late Davy Murray, we are indebted to the following photographers for the use of photographs from their collections – Rod Blencowe, Don Brundell, Colour-Rail, Peter Drummond, Dick Hardy, David Hunt, Shaz Lee, Phil Marsh, Bruce McCartney, Scott McGachy, David Murray, Ken Reid, Iain A. H. Smith, Peter Walker and David Wilcock.

A number of the photographs we have used have been gifted to us over the years and unfortunately we do not have the names of the photographers.

Despite a number of attempts, we have been unable to contact Geoff Green (responsible for the superb back cover photograph) or the family of the late Tam McKay, whose poem features, to seek permission to use these items. This will be corrected at the earliest opportunity if possible.

Thanks also to David Grant and Iain A. H. Smith for their help in tracking down the names and contact details of photographers.

Final thanks to our own Colin Cant for proofreading, Fraser Birrell for the mileage and Nick Swierklanski for our logo.